HOW TO PRAY ROSARY

Table of Content

INTRODUCTION	3
HISTORY OF THE ROSARY	4
THE POWER OF THE ROSARY	5
FAITH: NURTURING BELIEF AND TRUST	6
HOPE: FINDING STRENGTH IN UNCERTAINTY	8
LOVE: EMBRACING COMPASSION AND CHARITY	10
PATIENCE: CULTIVATING PERSEVERANCE AND SERENITY	12
HUMILITY: EMBODYING MODESTY AND GRATITUDE	14
FORGIVENESS: HEALING THROUGH MERCY AND RECONCILIATION	16
PURITY: CULTIVATING INNER WHOLENESS AND INTEGRITY	18
JOY: DISCOVERING THE GIFT OF GLADNESS AND CONTENTMENT	20
PEACE: NURTURING HARMONY AND TRANQUILITY	22
STRUCTURE AND COMPONENTS OF THE ROSARY	24
THE SIGN OF THE CROSS	24
THE APOSTLES' CREED	25

- THE OUR FATHER 27
- THE HAIL MARY 29
- THE GLORY BE 30
- THE FATIMA PRAYER 31
- THE JOYFUL MYSTERIES 32
- THE SORROWFUL MYSTERIES 33
- THE GLORIOUS MYSTERIES 34
- THE LUMINOUS MYSTERIES 35

ROSARY BEADS AND THEIR SIGNIFICANCE 36
HOW TO PRAY THE ROSARY STEP BY STEP 38
BENEFITS AND SPIRITUAL SIGNIFICANCE 40
MEDITATIVE AND CONTEMPLATIVE ASPECTS OF THE ROSARY 42
PROMOTING INNER PEACE AND SERENITY 44
INTERCESSORY POWER AND THE ROLE OF MARY 46
VARIATIONS AND ADAPTATIONS OF THE ROSARY 48
- CULTURAL AND REGIONAL DIFFERENCES 48
- SPECIALIZED VERSIONS FOR SPECIFIC INTENTIONS OR OCCASIONS 50
- POPULAR VARIATIONS IN DIFFERENT CATHOLIC COMMUNITIES 52

COMMON QUESTIONS AND MISCONCEPTIONS 54
- ADDRESSING COMMON DOUBTS AND CONCERNS ABOUT THE ROSARY: 56
- CLARIFYING MISCONCEPTIONS ABOUT THE ROSARY 58

TIPS FOR PRAYING THE ROSARY EFFECTIVELY 60
- CREATING A CONDUCIVE ENVIRONMENT FOR PRAYER 60
- DEVELOPING A PRAYER ROUTINE 61
- TECHNIQUES FOR MAINTAINING FOCUS AND CONCENTRATION 63

CONCLUSION 70

INTRODUCTION

The Rosary is a powerful and cherished prayer in the Catholic tradition, known for its profound spiritual significance and the virtues it cultivates in the lives of believers. Rooted in centuries of devotion, the Rosary holds a special place in the hearts of millions around the world. It is not only a means of offering prayers to the Blessed Virgin Mary but also a source of inspiration and guidance in living a virtuous life.

The Rosary serves as a source of strength and consolation during challenging times. Its repetitive nature and rhythmic prayers provide solace, peace, and a sense of connection to the Divine. In times of sorrow, anxiety, or uncertainty, the Rosary offers comfort and a refuge for the troubled soul. It becomes a means of seeking Mary's intercession, finding encouragement, and finding solace in the arms of our Heavenly Mother.

In this exploration of Rosary Virtues, we delve into the deep wellspring of spiritual wisdom and inspiration that the Rosary provides. Through the contemplation of the Mysteries and the embodiment of the virtues they illuminate, we are called to emulate the life of Christ and find solace in the gentle guidance of Mary. As we embark on this journey of reflection and growth, may the Rosary continue to nourish our souls and lead us closer to the divine virtues that shape our lives.

HISTORY OF THE ROSARY

The history of the Rosary is intertwined with the rich tapestry of Catholic devotion and piety. Its origins can be traced back to the early centuries of Christianity, although the specific details of its development are not entirely clear. Over time, the Rosary has evolved and gained prominence as a beloved prayer practice within the Catholic Church.

The roots of the Rosary can be found in the practice of praying the Psalms, which were recited by monks and religious communities. Laypeople that desired to participate in this form of prayer but were unable to memorize or read the Psalms began to substitute repetitive prayers, such as the Our Father and Hail Mary, to engage in a similar form of devotion.

During the medieval period, the Rosary as we know it today began to take shape. It is believed that the repetition of the Hail Mary prayer, combined with the use of beads for counting, was inspired by the monastic practice of praying the 150 Psalms using a string of beads. This new form of prayer became known as the "Psalter of Mary" or "Our Lady's Psalter."

One significant figure in the history of the Rosary is Saint Dominic, the founder of the Dominican Order. Tradition holds that the Blessed Virgin Mary appeared to him in the early 13th century and bestowed upon him the Rosary as a spiritual weapon against heresy and a means to convert souls. Saint Dominic then promoted the practice of the Rosary among the faithful, emphasizing its power as a tool for meditation and intercessory prayer.

In the 15th century, the Rosary underwent further development. The structure of the Rosary began to resemble its current form, with the division of the prayers into decades and the inclusion of the Mysteries. These Mysteries, reflecting on key moments in the life of Jesus and Mary, were meant to provide a framework for contemplation and deepen the spiritual experience of the Rosary.

In more recent times, particularly during the 20th century, several popes have emphasized the significance of the Rosary. Pope Leo XIII issued a series of encyclicals on the Rosary, calling it a powerful means of obtaining grace and expressing his own devotion to Mary. Pope Saint John Paul II, in his apostolic letter "Rosarium Virginis Mariae," introduced the Luminous Mysteries, further enriching the contemplation of the Rosary.

Today, the Rosary continues to hold a central place in Catholic spirituality. It is embraced by millions of faithful worldwide as a means of encountering the divine, seeking the intercession of the Blessed Mother, and growing in holiness.

THE POWER OF THE ROSARY

The Rosary is a prayer of immense power and significance within the Catholic tradition. It holds a special place in the hearts of believers, who attest to the transformative effects and spiritual benefits derived from its practice. The power of the Rosary lies in its ability to foster a deep connection with God, to draw upon the intercession of the Blessed Virgin Mary, and to cultivate virtues that shape the lives of those who pray it.

One of the primary sources of power in the Rosary is its capacity to facilitate a profound encounter with the divine. Through the repetition of prayers and the meditative reflection on the Mysteries, the Rosary leads individuals into a state of deep contemplation and spiritual communion. It creates a space for dialogue with God, enabling believers to pour out their hearts, express their gratitude, seek forgiveness, and present their petitions with faith and trust.

Moreover, the Rosary invokes the intercession of the Blessed Virgin Mary, who holds a unique and revered place in Catholic theology. Mary is regarded as the Mother of God, full of grace and endowed with a special role in salvation history. Praying the Rosary is an act of turning to Mary as a loving mother and entrusting one's intentions, needs, and struggles to her maternal care. It is believed that she intercedes on behalf of those who approach her with devotion, presenting their prayers before her Son, Jesus Christ.

The Rosary is also a powerful means of spiritual warfare and protection. It is seen as a spiritual weapon against evil, temptation, and the forces that seek to undermine faith. The act of praying the Rosary with faith and intentionality is believed to invoke God's grace and protection, dispelling darkness, and ushering in the light of Christ. It provides comfort, strength, and peace in times of trial, helping believers to navigate challenges and find solace in the arms of their Heavenly Mother.

The Rosary is intimately connected to the cultivation of virtues. As believers reflect on the Mysteries, they are invited to contemplate the virtues exemplified by Jesus and Mary. The Rosary serves as a school of virtue, nurturing qualities such as faith, hope, love, humility, obedience, patience, and compassion. Through the repetition and meditation on the prayers and Mysteries, the Rosary plants seeds of virtue within the hearts of those who pray it, gradually shaping their character and disposition.

Furthermore, the power of the Rosary extends beyond the individual practitioner. When the Rosary is prayed collectively, it fosters a sense of unity and communion among believers. It becomes a source of shared devotion, intercession, and spiritual support. Group recitation of the Rosary can create a powerful energy of prayer, amplifying its efficacy and impact.

FAITH: NURTURING BELIEF AND TRUST

Faith is a fundamental virtue that lies at the heart of the Christian life, and the Rosary serves as a powerful means of nurturing and deepening this essential aspect of spirituality. Faith involves believing in the unseen, trusting in God's providence, and surrendering to His divine will. Through the Rosary, believers are encouraged to cultivate a vibrant and living faith, fostering a profound sense of belief and trust in God.

When praying the Rosary, the faithful embark on a journey of faith as they contemplate the Mysteries and reflect upon the life, death, and resurrection of Jesus Christ. In the Joyful Mysteries, they witness the Annunciation and the birth of Jesus, marveling at the divine plan unfolding before their eyes. The Sorrowful Mysteries lead them to meditate on the suffering and sacrifice of Christ, prompting them to trust in the redemptive power of His love. The Glorious Mysteries inspire hope as they celebrate the triumph of the Resurrection and the promise of eternal life. The Luminous Mysteries illuminate the public ministry of Jesus, inviting believers to follow His teachings and place their trust in His guidance.

Through the repetition of prayers and the contemplation of the Mysteries, the Rosary invites individuals to nurture their belief in the truths of the Christian faith. It strengthens their conviction that God is present, active, and intimately involved in their lives. It instills confidence that He hears their prayers, guides their steps, and fulfills His promises. The Rosary becomes a conduit through which believers express their faith and seek to deepen their relationship with God.

Moreover, the Rosary encourages a spirit of trust in God's providence. As believers recite the Our Father prayer, they acknowledge God as their loving and caring Father, who provides for their needs. In praying the Hail Mary, they turn to the intercession of the Blessed Virgin Mary, trusting in her maternal care and guidance. The Rosary serves as a reminder that faith involves surrendering one's worries, fears, and anxieties into the hands of a loving God, knowing that He is faithful and will always provide.

The repetition of prayers in the Rosary helps to anchor faith in the hearts of believers. By reciting the same words and phrases, they reinforce the truths they profess, internalizing them and allowing them to penetrate deeply into their souls. The rhythmic nature of the Rosary creates a sense of peace and tranquility, allowing individuals to enter into a state of contemplation and connection with the divine. It provides a sacred space to nourish their faith, fostering a sense of awe, reverence, and humility before the mysteries of God's love.

In nurturing belief and trust, the Rosary becomes a powerful tool for the faithful to strengthen their faith, deepen their relationship with God, and find solace in times of doubt or uncertainty. It invites believers to embark on a journey of faith, embracing the mysteries of salvation and surrendering their hearts to the transformative power of divine grace. Through the Rosary, faith is nurtured and fortified, becoming a guiding light that illuminates the path of the faithful.

HOPE: FINDING STRENGTH IN UNCERTAINTY

Hope is a vital virtue that sustains and uplifts the human spirit, especially in times of uncertainty and adversity. Within the context of the Rosary, hope takes on a profound significance as believers reflect on the Mysteries and draw inspiration from the life and teachings of Jesus Christ. The Rosary becomes a source of strength, a beacon of light, and a reminder that even in the midst of challenges, hope can prevail.

As the faithful pray the Rosary, they encounter the Mysteries that encompass the entirety of Jesus' life: the Joyful, Sorrowful, Glorious, and Luminous Mysteries. Each set of Mysteries offers a unique opportunity to nurture hope and find solace in God's plan. In the Joyful Mysteries, hope is kindled as believers reflect on the Annunciation, the Nativity, and other moments that heralded the coming of the Savior. They witness the fulfillment of God's promises and are encouraged to trust in His providence.

In the Sorrowful Mysteries, hope is strengthened as believers meditate on the suffering and sacrifice of Jesus on the Cross. Despite the darkness and pain, the faithful find hope in the redemptive power of Christ's love, knowing that His sacrifice brings salvation and eternal life. The Glorious Mysteries affirm the triumph of hope as believers contemplate the Resurrection, Ascension, and the promise of Christ's return. These mysteries remind the faithful that no matter the challenges they face, hope in the ultimate victory of Christ remains steadfast.

The introduction of the Luminous Mysteries further enriches the Rosary's focus on hope. These mysteries invite believers to reflect on the public ministry of Jesus, which was marked by miracles, teachings, and the establishment of His kingdom. They remind the faithful that even in the midst of a broken world, hope can be found in the transformative power of Christ's message and the promise of His presence.

The repetitive nature of the Rosary prayers, combined with the meditative reflection on the Mysteries, fosters a deep sense of hope within the hearts of believers. The rhythm and familiarity of the prayers provide a comforting and reassuring cadence, allowing individuals to enter into a state of peaceful contemplation. In this space, hope is nurtured and fortified, as the faithful draw strength from their connection with God and the intercession of the Blessed Virgin Mary.

Moreover, the Rosary offers a tangible expression of hope within the Catholic community. When individuals pray the Rosary together, a sense of unity and shared hope is forged. The collective recitation of prayers creates a powerful energy that encourages and supports one another. It reminds believers that they are not alone in their struggles, and that hope can be multiplied through the communion of saints and the support of fellow pilgrims on the journey of faith.

In times of uncertainty, the Rosary becomes a refuge, a source of comfort, and a reminder that hope is not merely wishful thinking, but a firm belief in the goodness and faithfulness of God. It encourages the faithful to trust in God's plan, to embrace the promises of Christ, and to find strength in the hope that transcends temporal challenges. Through the Rosary, believers find solace, inspiration, and renewed confidence to face the trials of life, knowing that hope is an anchor for the soul, steadfast and sure.

LOVE: EMBRACING COMPASSION AND CHARITY

Love is at the core of the Christian message, and the Rosary provides a profound opportunity to cultivate and embody this transformative virtue. Through the prayers and meditations of the Rosary, believers are invited to embrace compassion and charity, following the example of Jesus Christ and the Blessed Virgin Mary.

In the Mysteries of the Rosary, love is vividly portrayed. The Joyful Mysteries invite believers to reflect on the Annunciation, the Visitation, and the birth of Jesus, where love is seen in the selfless obedience of Mary and the divine gift of God's love to humanity. The Sorrowful Mysteries depict the love of Christ through His Passion, Crucifixion, and Death, revealing His sacrificial love for all humankind. The Glorious Mysteries celebrate the Resurrection, Ascension, and the outpouring of the Holy Spirit, demonstrating the power of love to conquer death and transform lives. The Luminous Mysteries showcase the love of Christ through His teachings, miracles, and the institution of the Eucharist, inviting believers to love one another as He has loved them.

Through the repetition of the Hail Mary prayer, believers invoke the intercession of the Blessed Virgin Mary, who embodies a profound love and compassion. Mary's presence in the Mysteries of the Rosary serves as a model of love, humility, and maternal care. Praying the Rosary encourages believers to emulate her example by embracing compassion and charity in their own lives, extending love to others as Mary did to her Son and all humanity.

The Rosary also fosters love through its transformative power. As believers engage in the prayers and meditations, the Rosary becomes a vehicle for encountering God's love and allowing it to permeate their hearts. It opens a space for believers to receive God's love and grace, which empowers them to love others selflessly. The repetition of the prayers creates a rhythm that helps individuals to enter into a state of contemplation, connecting with the divine source of love and allowing it to flow through them.

The Rosary nurtures the virtue of love by fostering a sense of community and unity among believers. When individuals pray the Rosary together, whether in a family setting or as part of a larger group, they are united in a common expression of love and devotion. The shared experience of praying the Rosary can deepen bonds of love and strengthen the sense of belonging to the larger family of God.

Furthermore, the Rosary inspires acts of charity and compassion. As believers meditate on the Mysteries, they are called to reflect on the practical implications of God's love in their lives. The Rosary invites them to consider how they can live out their faith through acts of kindness, mercy, and service to others. It encourages believers to extend love to those in need, to be instruments of God's compassion in the world.

In a world often marked by division and discord, the Rosary serves as a powerful reminder of the transformative power of love. It teaches believers to approach others with kindness, empathy, and understanding. Through the Rosary, believers are called to love not only those close to them but also their enemies, as Jesus instructed. It challenges them to embrace a radical love that transcends boundaries, seeks reconciliation, and promotes unity.

In praying the Rosary, believers are invited to embody the virtue of love and to become vessels of God's love in the world. It encourages them to grow in compassion, extend acts of charity, and foster unity among all people. The Rosary serves as a gentle guide, reminding believers that love is not merely a sentiment but a transformative force that can heal, restore, and bring forth the Kingdom of God on earth.

PATIENCE: CULTIVATING PERSEVERANCE AND SERENITY

Patience is a virtue that holds great significance in the Christian life, and the Rosary serves as a powerful means of cultivating and nurturing this essential quality. In a fast-paced and often turbulent world, the Rosary invites believers to embrace patience, fostering a spirit of perseverance and serenity in the face of challenges.

As believers engage in the repetitive prayers of the Rosary, they are reminded of the importance of patience. The rhythm of the prayers, the cadence of the beads, and the meditative reflection on the Mysteries create a space for stillness and tranquility. Through this repetitive and contemplative practice, the Rosary cultivates a patient disposition, allowing individuals to quiet their minds, calm their hearts, and find peace in the presence of God.

The Mysteries of the Rosary provide numerous examples of patience to reflect upon. In the Joyful Mysteries, believers witness the patient trust of Mary as she embraces God's plan, despite the uncertainties and challenges she faced. The Sorrowful Mysteries reveal the patience of Jesus as He endures the agony of His Passion and Crucifixion, displaying unwavering perseverance in fulfilling His mission of redemption. The Glorious Mysteries highlight the patience and hope of the disciples as they awaited the fulfillment of Christ's promise in the Resurrection and the coming of the Holy Spirit. The Luminous Mysteries emphasize the patient and steadfast teachings of Jesus, inviting believers to patiently follow His guidance.

Through the repetition and contemplation of the Rosary, believers are encouraged to apply the lessons of patience found in the Mysteries to their own lives. The Rosary becomes a training ground for perseverance and serenity. It teaches believers to trust in God's timing, to surrender control, and to patiently endure challenges, knowing that God's plans unfold in His perfect wisdom.

In a world marked by instant gratification and impatience, the Rosary offers a counter-cultural practice that invites believers to slow down, to be present, and to cultivate a patient attitude. It reminds them that some things in life require time, effort, and trust in God's providence. The repetitive nature of the Rosary prayers provides an opportunity to practice patience by engaging in the same prayers again and again, allowing the mind and heart to enter into a state of receptivity, openness, and surrender.

Moreover, the Rosary fosters serenity amidst the busyness and challenges of life. By entering into the contemplative space of the Rosary, believers find a refuge from the distractions and anxieties of the world. The repetition of the prayers creates a sense of rhythm and peace, enabling individuals to let go of restlessness and find tranquility in the presence of God. The Rosary becomes a pathway to serenity, grounding the faithful in the assurance that God is with them and that His peace surpasses all understanding.

In cultivating patience through the Rosary, believers develop a resilience that enables them to navigate the trials and tribulations of life with grace and perseverance. Patience allows them to endure setbacks, setbacks, and delays without losing hope or becoming disheartened. It fosters an attitude of trust in God's providence and an understanding that His timing is perfect.

The Rosary serves as a gentle teacher, guiding believers to embrace patience as they journey through the Mysteries and encounter the virtues displayed by Jesus and Mary. It invites individuals to surrender their impatience, to release their worries, and to find solace in the patient and loving presence of God.

HUMILITY: EMBODYING MODESTY AND GRATITUDE

Humility is a virtue of great significance in the Christian life, and the Rosary serves as a powerful means of cultivating and embodying this essential quality. Through the prayers and meditations of the Rosary, believers are invited to embrace humility, fostering a spirit of modesty and gratitude in their relationship with God and others.

As believers engage in the humble act of reciting the Rosary, they are reminded of their dependence on God and their need for His grace. The repetition of prayers and the contemplation of the Mysteries create a space for introspection and self-reflection. In this sacred space, the Rosary cultivates a humble disposition, helping individuals to recognize their limitations, acknowledge their faults, and surrender their ego to the loving will of God.

The Mysteries of the Rosary provide profound examples of humility to reflect upon. In the Joyful Mysteries, believers witness the humble acceptance of Mary as she responds to God's plan with modesty and obedience. The Sorrowful Mysteries reveal the humility of Jesus as He willingly undergoes suffering and death for the salvation of humanity. The Glorious Mysteries showcase the humility of the disciples as they proclaim the Resurrection and embrace their role in spreading the Gospel. The Luminous Mysteries emphasize the humility of Jesus as He engages in the ministry of service and calls His followers to a life of humility.

Through the repetition and contemplation of the Rosary, believers are encouraged to embrace humility in their own lives. The Rosary becomes a transformative practice that helps individuals to let go of pride, to cultivate modesty, and to recognize the value and dignity of every person. It teaches believers to place their trust in God, acknowledging that everything they have is a gift from Him.

The Rosary invites believers to practice gratitude as a form of humility. In each Hail Mary prayer, the faithful express gratitude to Mary for her intercession and to God for His blessings. This expression of gratitude helps individuals to develop a humble heart that recognizes their dependence on God and acknowledges His goodness and generosity.

Moreover, the Rosary fosters a sense of modesty and detachment from worldly pursuits. As individuals engage in the repetition of prayers, they are reminded of the fleeting nature of earthly accomplishments and the need to prioritize the eternal. The Rosary becomes a spiritual practice that helps believers detach themselves from excessive self-focus and material possessions, enabling them to embrace a spirit of simplicity and modesty.

In a world often driven by self-promotion and the pursuit of personal gain, the Rosary offers a counter-cultural practice that invites believers to embrace humility and to honor the dignity of every person. The repetitive nature of the prayers humbles the heart, leading individuals to recognize their own limitations and shortcomings. It becomes a pathway to self-awareness and self-reflection, nurturing an attitude of modesty and a willingness to serve others.

The Rosary also fosters gratitude, helping believers to appreciate the blessings in their lives and to acknowledge the grace and goodness of God. Gratitude is an expression of humility, recognizing that every good gift comes from above. The Rosary encourages believers to cultivate a grateful heart, even in the midst of challenges, trusting in God's providence and goodness.

Through the practice of the Rosary, humility becomes a transformative virtue that infuses daily life with a deep sense of modesty, gratitude, and reverence. The Rosary serves as a gentle guide, leading believers to embrace humility as they journey through the Mysteries and encounter the virtues displayed by Jesus and Mary. It invites individuals to surrender their pride, to foster a spirit of modesty, and to live in gratitude for the abundant blessings bestowed upon them. Through the humble practice of the Rosary, believers are inspired to walk in the footsteps of Christ, embodying the transformative power of humility in their lives.

FORGIVENESS: HEALING THROUGH MERCY AND RECONCILIATION

Forgiveness is a powerful virtue that lies at the heart of the Christian message, and the Rosary serves as a means of cultivating and embracing this transformative quality. Through the prayers and meditations of the Rosary, believers are invited to engage in the process of healing, mercy, and reconciliation, both in their relationship with God and with others.

As believers recite the Rosary, they encounter the Mysteries that depict the immense forgiveness and mercy of God. The Joyful Mysteries invite reflection on the Annunciation and the Incarnation, reminding believers of God's willingness to enter into the brokenness of humanity in order to offer forgiveness and reconciliation. The Sorrowful Mysteries reveal the depth of God's mercy as Jesus undergoes His Passion and Crucifixion, forgiving those who persecuted Him and reconciling humanity to God. The Glorious Mysteries celebrate the Resurrection, highlighting the power of forgiveness to conquer sin and restore relationships. The Luminous Mysteries emphasize the mercy of God as believers reflect on Jesus' invitation to repentance and reconciliation.

Through the repetition and contemplation of the Rosary, believers are encouraged to embrace forgiveness in their own lives. The Rosary becomes a transformative practice that helps individuals to release grudges, resentments, and the burden of unforgiveness. It fosters a spirit of mercy and reconciliation, inviting believers to follow the example of Jesus and extend forgiveness to others as they have been forgiven.

The Rosary teaches believers that forgiveness is a choice—an act of the will—and not necessarily dependent on feelings. It involves letting go of the desire for revenge or holding onto past hurts, and instead, opening oneself to the healing power of God's love and mercy. The repetitive prayers of the Rosary create a space for believers to surrender their pain and woundedness, allowing God's grace to work within them, transforming their hearts and enabling them to extend forgiveness to others.

Moreover, the Rosary nurtures a spirit of reconciliation, emphasizing the importance of seeking harmony and unity in relationships. It prompts believers to reflect on the ways in which they may have contributed to conflicts or divisions and invites them to take steps towards reconciliation, guided by the principles of mercy and love. The Rosary becomes a pathway to healing broken relationships, fostering understanding, and promoting peace.

In a world often marked by discord and brokenness, the Rosary offers a transformative practice that invites believers to embrace forgiveness, mercy, and reconciliation. It teaches that forgiveness is not a sign of weakness but an act of strength, allowing individuals to break free from the chains of bitterness and resentment. The Rosary fosters a spirit of humility, reminding believers that they too are in need of forgiveness and that God's mercy is abundant and available to all.

Through the practice of the Rosary, forgiveness becomes a transformative force that brings healing, restoration, and unity. The Rosary serves as a gentle guide, leading believers to embrace forgiveness as they journey through the Mysteries and encounter the virtues displayed by Jesus and Mary. It invites individuals to release the burden of unforgiveness, to extend mercy and reconciliation, and to experience the liberating power of forgiveness in their own lives and relationships. Through the transformative practice of the Rosary, believers are inspired to walk in the footsteps of Christ, embodying the healing and reconciling power of forgiveness.

PURITY: CULTIVATING INNER WHOLENESS AND INTEGRITY

P urity is a virtue of great significance in the Christian tradition, and the Rosary serves as a powerful means of cultivating and embracing this transformative quality. Through the prayers and meditations of the Rosary, believers are invited to cultivate inner wholeness, integrity, and a purity of heart.

As believers engage in the recitation of the Rosary, they are reminded of the importance of purity in their thoughts, words, and actions. The repetition of prayers and the contemplation of the Mysteries create a sacred space for introspection and self-reflection. In this space, the Rosary helps individuals to recognize and reject anything that compromises their inner purity and integrity, fostering a commitment to live in accordance with God's standards.

The Mysteries of the Rosary provide profound examples of purity to reflect upon. In the Joyful Mysteries, believers witness the purity of Mary's heart and her profound obedience to God's will. The Sorrowful Mysteries reveal the purity of Jesus' love as He endures suffering and death for the redemption of humanity. The Glorious Mysteries celebrate the purity of the Resurrection, emphasizing the triumph of purity over sin and death. The Luminous Mysteries highlight the purity of Jesus' teachings and invite believers to embrace a purity of mind, heart, and action in their own lives.

Through the repetition and contemplation of the Rosary, believers are encouraged to embrace purity in their thoughts, words, and deeds. The Rosary becomes a transformative practice that helps individuals guard their minds against impure thoughts, choose their words with integrity and kindness, and act in ways that honor God and reflect His purity. It instills a desire for holiness and encourages individuals to cultivate a life of virtue and moral integrity.

The Rosary teaches believers to seek purity not only in their actions but also in their intentions and motivations. It calls for a sincere examination of conscience, challenging individuals to root out any hidden areas of impurity or hypocrisy. The repetitive prayers create a space for individuals to acknowledge their weaknesses, seek forgiveness, and resolve to live with integrity and purity.

Moreover, the Rosary fosters purity of heart and fosters a deep sense of devotion and reverence for God. Through the contemplation of the Mysteries, believers are drawn into a profound encounter with the life, death, and resurrection of Jesus Christ. This encounter nurtures a love for

God and a desire to conform one's heart to His purity. The Rosary becomes a pathway to a deeper relationship with God, guiding believers towards a life of holiness and purity.

In a world often marked by moral compromise and impurity, the Rosary offers a transformative practice that invites believers to embrace purity, integrity, and wholeness. The repetition of prayers helps to guard the mind against impure influences, nurturing a culture of purity in thought and word. The Rosary fosters a spirit of self-discipline and self-control, allowing individuals to resist the allure of temptation and to choose actions that honor God and reflect His purity.

Through the practice of the Rosary, purity becomes a transformative virtue that brings inner wholeness, integrity, and alignment with God's will. The Rosary serves as a gentle guide, leading believers to embrace purity as they journey through the Mysteries and encounter the virtues displayed by Jesus and Mary. It invites individuals to seek God's grace and mercy, to purify their hearts, and to experience the liberating power of living a life of purity and integrity. Through the transformative practice of the Rosary, believers are inspired to walk in the footsteps of Christ, embodying the purity and holiness that leads to true fulfillment and joy.

JOY: DISCOVERING THE GIFT OF GLADNESS AND CONTENTMENT

Joy is a profound virtue that resonates deeply within the Christian faith, and the Rosary serves as a means of discovering and embracing this transformative quality. Through the prayers and meditations of the Rosary, believers are invited to cultivate joy, embracing a sense of gladness and contentment that stems from a deep relationship with God.

As believers engage in the recitation of the Rosary, they are reminded of the abiding joy that comes from knowing and loving God. The repetition of prayers and the contemplation of the Mysteries create a space for deep reflection and spiritual connection. In this sacred space, the Rosary nurtures a sense of joy that transcends circumstances and anchors believers in the unchanging goodness and love of God.

The Mysteries of the Rosary provide profound examples of joy to reflect upon. In the Joyful Mysteries, believers witness the joy that radiates from Mary's heart as she receives the angelic message and carries the Son of God within her. The Sorrowful Mysteries reveal the transformative joy that emerges from Jesus' sacrifice and the hope it brings for the redemption of humanity. The Glorious Mysteries celebrate the uncontainable joy of the Resurrection and the promise of eternal life. The Luminous Mysteries highlight the joy that comes from encountering the truth of God's teachings and the transformation it brings to hearts and minds.

Through the repetition and contemplation of the Rosary, believers are encouraged to embrace joy in their own lives. The Rosary becomes a transformative practice that helps individuals to shift their focus from temporary circumstances to the eternal reality of God's love and providence. It fosters an attitude of gratitude and contentment, allowing individuals to find joy in the simple blessings of life and in their relationship with God.

The Rosary teaches believers that true joy is not dependent on external circumstances but is rooted in a deep and abiding relationship with God. It invites believers to surrender their worries, fears, and anxieties to God and to trust in His loving care. The repetitive prayers of the Rosary create a space for individuals to let go of negativity and embrace a mindset of joy and gratitude, fostering a spirit of contentment and gladness.

Moreover, the Rosary fosters joy by nurturing a sense of connection and communion with God and the communion of saints. Through the contemplation of the Mysteries, believers enter into a profound encounter with the life, death, and resurrection of Jesus Christ. This encounter nurtures a love for God and a sense of belonging to the larger family of faith. The Rosary becomes a pathway to a deeper relationship with God, guiding believers towards a life of joy that is grounded in their connection to the divine.

In a world often marked by restlessness and discontentment, the Rosary offers a transformative practice that invites believers to embrace joy and find fulfillment in their relationship with God. The repetition of prayers helps to still the mind, quiet the heart, and open the soul to the presence of God. The Rosary fosters an attitude of praise and thanksgiving, allowing individuals to find joy in the gift of life, in the beauty of creation, and in the hope of eternal salvation.

Through the practice of the Rosary, joy becomes a transformative virtue that brings deep gladness, contentment, and an abiding sense of God's presence. The Rosary serves as a gentle guide, leading believers to embrace joy as they journey through the Mysteries and encounter the virtues displayed by Jesus and Mary. It invites individuals to surrender their worries, to embrace gratitude, and to experience the transformative power of joy in their own lives. Through the transformative practice of the Rosary, believers are inspired to walk in the footsteps of Christ, embodying the joy that comes from a life rooted in God's love.

PEACE: NURTURING HARMONY AND TRANQUILITY

Peace is a precious virtue that resonates deeply within the Christian faith, and the Rosary serves as a powerful means of nurturing and embracing this transformative quality. Through the prayers and meditations of the Rosary, believers are invited to cultivate peace, fostering a spirit of harmony and tranquility in their relationship with God and others.

As believers engage in the recitation of the Rosary, they are reminded of the peace that comes from knowing and trusting in God's presence and providence. The repetition of prayers and the contemplation of the Mysteries create a space for stillness and reflection. In this sacred space, the Rosary nurtures a deep sense of peace that surpasses understanding and anchors believers in the unchanging love and peace of God.

The Mysteries of the Rosary provide profound examples of peace to reflect upon. In the Joyful Mysteries, believers witness the peaceful surrender of Mary to God's plan and the peace that radiates from the presence of the Infant Jesus. The Sorrowful Mysteries reveal the transformative peace that emerges from Jesus' embrace of suffering and His ultimate triumph over sin and death. The Glorious Mysteries celebrate the peace that comes from the Resurrection and the promise of eternal life. The Luminous Mysteries highlight the peace that flows from encountering the truth of God's teachings and following the path of righteousness.

Through the repetition and contemplation of the Rosary, believers are encouraged to embrace peace in their own lives. The Rosary becomes a transformative practice that helps individuals to release their anxieties, worries, and burdens to God, and to find rest and tranquility in His loving embrace. It fosters an attitude of surrender and trust, allowing individuals to experience peace in the midst of life's challenges and uncertainties.

The Rosary teaches believers that true peace is not found in external circumstances but in an intimate relationship with God. It invites believers to quiet their minds and hearts, to let go of restless striving, and to enter into a state of surrender and receptivity. The repetitive prayers of the Rosary create a space for individuals to seek peace, to be still in God's presence, and to experience the transformative power of His peace.

Moreover, the Rosary fosters peace by nurturing a sense of connection and communion with God and the communion of saints. Through the contemplation of the Mysteries, believers enter into a profound encounter with the life, death, and resurrection of Jesus Christ. This encounter nurtures a love for God and a sense of belonging to the larger family of faith. The Rosary becomes a pathway to a deeper relationship with God, guiding believers towards a life of peace that is rooted in their connection to the divine.

In a world often marked by turmoil and unrest, the Rosary offers a transformative practice that invites believers to embrace peace and seek harmony in their lives. The repetition of prayers helps to still the mind, calm the heart, and create an inner space for God's peace to dwell. The Rosary fosters an attitude of surrender and serenity, allowing individuals to find peace in the midst of challenges, to respond to conflicts with grace and forgiveness, and to cultivate harmonious relationships.

Through the practice of the Rosary, peace becomes a transformative virtue that brings deep tranquility, harmony, and an abiding sense of God's presence. The Rosary serves as a gentle guide, leading believers to embrace peace as they journey through the Mysteries and encounter the virtues displayed by Jesus and Mary. It invites individuals to surrender their anxieties, to trust in God's providence, and to experience the transformative power of His peace in their own lives. Through the transformative practice of the Rosary, believers are inspired to walk in the footsteps of Christ, embodying the peace that surpasses all understanding and becomes a beacon of hope in the world.

STRUCTURE AND COMPONENTS OF THE ROSARY

The Rosary is a structured prayer that consists of several components, each serving a specific purpose in guiding believers through the Mysteries of the faith. Understanding the structure and components of the Rosary can deepen one's experience and facilitate a more meaningful practice.

The Rosary is comprised of specific prayers and meditations known as the Mysteries. These prayers and Mysteries guide believers through the life, death, and resurrection of Jesus Christ, inviting them to reflect on the significant events and teachings of His earthly journey. The prayers and Mysteries are repeated and contemplated in a specific sequence, creating a rhythmic and meditative experience.

PRAYERS AND MYSTERIES

THE SIGN OF THE CROSS

The Sign of the Cross is a fundamental gesture that initiates and concludes the recitation of the Rosary. It is a simple yet profound act of devotion that reminds believers of the presence of the Holy Trinity—God the Father, God the Son, and God the Holy Spirit—in their prayerful journey.

To make the Sign of the Cross, believers use their right hand to touch their forehead, chest, left shoulder, and right shoulder while saying the words, "In the name of the Father, and of the Son, and of the Holy Spirit. Amen." This gesture symbolizes the belief in the Triune God and invokes His blessings and guidance.

The Sign of the Cross is a powerful reminder of the Christian faith and the redemptive work of Jesus Christ. By tracing the cross upon themselves, believers affirm their identity as followers of Christ and acknowledge His sacrifice on the cross for their salvation. It serves as a unifying symbol for believers, connecting them to the universal Church and the communion of saints.

In the context of the Rosary, the Sign of the Cross is made at the beginning and end of the prayer. It signifies the believers' desire to approach God with reverence and openness, seeking His presence and guidance throughout the recitation of the Rosary. It acts as a spiritual threshold, inviting believers to enter into a sacred space of prayer and contemplation.

The Sign of the Cross also acts as a reminder of the Trinitarian nature of the Christian faith. By invoking the name of the Father, Son, and Holy Spirit, believers acknowledge the divine presence in their prayer and express their dependence on God's grace and love.

This simple yet profound gesture encapsulates the essence of the Christian faith and serves as a foundational act of devotion in the recitation of the Rosary. It grounds believers in their relationship with the Triune God and sets the tone for their prayerful encounter with Him throughout the Mysteries.

THE APOSTLES' CREED

The Apostles' Creed is a statement of faith that holds great significance within the Christian tradition. It is a concise summary of the core beliefs of Christianity and serves as a foundation for the prayers that follow in the Rosary. Reciting the Apostles' Creed unites believers in their shared beliefs and affirms their commitment to the teachings of Jesus Christ.

The Apostles' Creed derives its name from the belief that it represents the faith professed by the apostles, who were chosen by Jesus to be His closest followers and witnesses to His life, death, and resurrection. The creed embodies the essential doctrines of the Christian faith and provides a succinct proclamation of the fundamental beliefs held by Christians worldwide.

The Apostles' Creed affirms belief in God as the Father Almighty, the Creator of heaven and earth. It acknowledges Jesus Christ as His only Son, our Lord, who was conceived by the Holy Spirit, born of the Virgin Mary, suffered under Pontius Pilate, was crucified, died, and was buried. The creed also proclaims His descent into hell, His resurrection on the third day, His ascension into heaven, and His coming again to judge the living and the dead.

RECITATION OF THE APOSTLES' CREED

I believe in God, the Father Almighty,

Creator of heaven and earth

I believe in Jesus Christ, His only Son, our Lord,

Who was conceived by the Holy Spirit

Born of the Virgin Mary,

Suffered under Pontius Pilate,

Was crucified, died, and was buried;

He descended to the dead.

On the third day, He rose again;

He ascended into heaven,

He is seated at the right hand of the Father,

And He will come to judge the living and the dead.

I believe in the Holy Spirit,

The holy Catholic Church,

The communion of saints,

The forgiveness of sins,

The resurrection of the body,

And the life everlasting

Amen

THE OUR FATHER

The Our Father, also known as the Lord's Prayer, is a central Christian prayer that was taught by Jesus to his disciples. It holds a significant place in Christian worship and is considered a model prayer. The prayer is found in the New Testament of the Bible, specifically in the Gospel of Matthew (Matthew 6:9-13) and the Gospel of Luke (Luke 11:2-4).

The Our Father is a prayer addressed to God the Father, expressing reverence, adoration, and a desire for His will to be done. It consists of several key components:

Addressing God: The prayer begins by addressing God as "Our Father." This highlights the personal relationship between God and believers, emphasizing the idea of God as a loving and caring Father.

Praise and Worship: The prayer acknowledges and glorifies God's holiness and greatness with the words, "Hallowed be your name." This portion of the prayer expresses reverence and adoration for God.

Petitions for God's Kingdom: The prayer seeks the coming of God's kingdom and the fulfillment of His will on earth, just as it is in heaven. This represents the desire for God's rule and the establishment of His divine plan.

Daily Bread: The prayer includes a request for daily sustenance, symbolizing both physical and spiritual nourishment. It reflects the acknowledgment of our dependence on God for our needs.

Forgiveness and Mercy: The prayer emphasizes the importance of forgiveness by asking God to forgive our trespasses, just as we forgive those who have wronged us. It highlights the need for reconciliation and the cultivation of a forgiving spirit.

Protection from Temptation: The prayer seeks God's guidance and strength to overcome temptation and to deliver believers from evil. It acknowledges the presence of challenges and seeks divine assistance to remain faithful.

RECITATION OF THE OUR FATHER

Our Father, who art in heaven,

Hallowed be thy Name,

Thy kingdom come,

Thy will be done,

On earth as it is in heaven.

Give us this day our daily bread.

And forgive us our trespasses,

As we forgive those

Who trespass against us.

And lead us not into temptation,

But deliver us from evil.

For thine is the kingdom,

And the power, and the glory,

Forever and ever

Amen.

THE HAIL MARY

The Hail Mary is a traditional Catholic prayer that honors the Virgin Mary and seeks her intercession. It is composed of two parts: the first part is a greeting by the angel Gabriel to Mary, and the second part is a request for Mary's prayers.

RECITATION OF THE HAIL MARY

> "Hail Mary, full of grace,
>
> The Lord is with thee;
>
> Blessed art thou among women,
>
> And blessed is the fruit of thy womb, Jesus.
>
> Holy Mary, Mother of God,
>
> Pray for us sinners,
>
> Now and at the hour of our death
>
> Amen.

The first part of the prayer is taken from the biblical account of the Annunciation, where the angel Gabriel greets Mary with the words "Hail, full of grace, the Lord is with thee" (Luke 1:28). This acknowledges Mary's unique role in God's plan of salvation.

The second part of the prayer asks for Mary's intercession and prayer on behalf of sinners. It acknowledges Mary as the Mother of God and seeks her help and protection. Catholics believe that Mary, being close to Jesus, has a special role in interceding for us before her Son.

The Hail Mary is a central prayer in the Rosary, and it is repeated multiple times during the recitation of each decade. It is a way to honor Mary and seek her powerful intercession as we meditate on the life and teachings of Jesus.

THE GLORY BE

The Glory Be, also known as the "Doxology" or the "Gloria Patri," is a short prayer that gives praise and glory to the Holy Trinity: God the Father, God the Son (Jesus Christ), and God the Holy Spirit. It is a common prayer in Christian worship and is often recited during the Rosary and other devotional practices.

RECITATION OF THE GLORY BE

> "Glory be to the Father,
>
> And to the Son,
>
> And to the Holy Spirit
>
> As it was in the beginning,
>
> Is now and ever shall be,
>
> World without end
>
> Amen."

The Glory Be acknowledges the eternal nature and unity of the Holy Trinity. It starts by glorifying the Father, recognizing His divine authority and sovereignty. Then it gives equal praise to the Son, Jesus Christ, who is considered the second person of the Trinity and the Savior of humanity. Finally, it honors the Holy Spirit, the third person of the Trinity, who is believed to guide and empower believers.

The closing phrase, "As it was in the beginning, is now, and ever shall be, world without end," emphasizes the eternal nature of God's glory and presence. It expresses the belief that God's glory has always existed, continues to exist, and will exist forever.

The Glory Be is a simple yet powerful prayer that highlights the central doctrine of the Holy Trinity and invites believers to offer praise and honor to God in all His three persons.

THE FATIMA PRAYER

The Fatima Prayer, also known as the "O My Jesus" prayer, is a prayer that is associated with the apparitions of the Virgin Mary in Fatima, Portugal, in 1917. According to the accounts of the three shepherd children who witnessed these apparitions, the prayer was revealed by Mary during one of her visits. It has since become a popular part of the Rosary and other Catholic devotions.

RECITATION OF THE FATIMA PRAYER:

> "O my Jesus, forgive us our sins,
>
> Save us from the fires of hell,
>
> Lead all souls to heaven,
>
> Especially those in most need of Thy mercy. Amen."

The Fatima Prayer is a petition to Jesus, seeking forgiveness for sins and salvation from the fires of hell. It expresses a deep concern for the eternal destiny of souls and a desire for their salvation. It reflects the belief that Jesus is the ultimate source of mercy and redemption.

The prayer also specifically mentions the desire to lead all souls to heaven, emphasizing the universal scope of God's mercy and the hope for the salvation of all. It includes a special plea for those who are in most need of God's mercy, highlighting the compassionate nature of this prayer.

The Fatima Prayer serves as a reminder of the messages and requests conveyed by the Virgin Mary during the Fatima apparitions, which included the call for prayer, penance, and conversion. It is often recited at the end of each decade of the Rosary as an additional prayer for the intentions of those in need and for the salvation of souls.

THE JOYFUL MYSTERIES

The Joyful Mysteries are a set of meditations or events from the life of Jesus and Mary that are traditionally prayed as part of the Rosary. These mysteries focus on joyful events and highlight significant moments in the early life of Jesus. The Joyful Mysteries consist of the following five mysteries:

- The Annunciation: This mystery reflects on the angel Gabriel's visit to the Virgin Mary, announcing that she would conceive a child by the power of the Holy Spirit. Mary humbly accepts God's plan and becomes the Mother of Jesus.
- The Visitation: In this mystery, Mary visits her relative Elizabeth, who is pregnant with John the Baptist. The encounter is filled with joy as both women express their faith and share in the anticipation of the miraculous events unfolding in their lives.
- The Nativity: This mystery commemorates the birth of Jesus in Bethlehem. Mary and Joseph find shelter in a humble stable, and Jesus is born, bringing hope and salvation to the world. The shepherds and angels also play a significant role in this joyous event.
- The Presentation: Mary and Joseph present the infant Jesus in the temple, as was the Jewish custom. They encounter Simeon, a devout and righteous man who had been waiting for the Messiah. Simeon recognizes Jesus as the fulfillment of God's promise and offers a prophetic blessing.
- The Finding of Jesus in the Temple: This mystery recounts an incident when Jesus, as a young boy, goes missing during a visit to Jerusalem. After searching anxiously, Mary and Joseph find Jesus in the temple, conversing with the teachers. This event highlights Jesus' unique wisdom and His mission as the Son of God.

The Joyful Mysteries invite believers to reflect on the joy and wonder associated with the early life of Jesus and Mary. Through these meditations, one can contemplate the faith, humility, and obedience demonstrated by Mary and Joseph, as well as the joy and blessings brought by the birth and presence of Jesus in the world.

THE SORROWFUL MYSTERIES

The Sorrowful Mysteries are a set of meditations or events from the life of Jesus that are traditionally prayed as part of the Rosary. These mysteries focus on the suffering and passion of Jesus leading up to His crucifixion. The Sorrowful Mysteries consist of the following five mysteries:

- The Agony in the Garden: This mystery reflects on Jesus' prayerful agony in the Garden of Gethsemane. Knowing the suffering that awaited Him, Jesus prays to the Father, expressing His anguish and surrendering to God's will.
- The Scourging at the Pillar: In this mystery, Jesus is cruelly scourged and whipped by Roman soldiers. He endures intense physical pain and humiliation, bearing the weight of humanity's sins upon Himself.
- The Crowning with Thorns: This mystery recalls the mocking and crowning of Jesus with thorns by the soldiers. They taunt Him, inflicting further suffering both physically and emotionally.
- The Carrying of the Cross: Jesus carries His cross along the Via Dolorosa, the path to Calvary. This arduous journey symbolizes the immense burden of sin that Jesus bears for humanity's redemption.
- The Crucifixion: The final sorrowful mystery centers on Jesus' crucifixion on Mount Calvary. He willingly accepts this ultimate act of sacrifice, offering Himself as the perfect atonement for the sins of humanity. Mary, the mother of Jesus, stands at the foot of the cross, sharing in His pain and offering her support and love.

The Sorrowful Mysteries invite believers to reflect on the immense suffering and selfless love demonstrated by Jesus during His passion and crucifixion. Through these meditations, one can contemplate the depth of Jesus' sacrifice and the extent of God's love for humanity. It is an opportunity to express gratitude, seek forgiveness, and unite one's own sufferings with the redemptive suffering of Jesus.

THE GLORIOUS MYSTERIES

The Glorious Mysteries are a set of meditations or events from the life of Jesus and Mary that are traditionally prayed as part of the Rosary. These mysteries focus on the glorious events that followed Jesus' resurrection and emphasize the triumph of life over death. The Glorious Mysteries consist of the following five mysteries:

- The Resurrection: This mystery commemorates Jesus' triumph over death. After His crucifixion and burial, Jesus rises from the dead on the third day, conquering sin and offering the promise of eternal life to all who believe in Him.
- The Ascension: In this mystery, Jesus ascends into heaven forty days after His resurrection. He returns to His Father, gloriously taking His place at the right hand of God, while promising to send the Holy Spirit to guide and empower His followers.
- The Descent of the Holy Spirit: This mystery recalls the coming of the Holy Spirit upon the disciples at Pentecost. The Holy Spirit, in the form of tongues of fire, descends upon the apostles, empowering them to proclaim the Gospel fearlessly and to establish the early Church.
- The Assumption: This mystery celebrates the Assumption of the Virgin Mary, body and soul, into heaven. Mary, who was sinless and full of grace, is taken up into glory by God as a sign of her unique role in the plan of salvation and as a promise of our own resurrection and glorification.
- The Coronation: The final glorious mystery focuses on the Coronation of the Blessed Virgin Mary as Queen of Heaven and Earth. Mary, having faithfully fulfilled her mission on earth, is crowned by her Son, Jesus, as a reflection of her supreme intercessory role and her special place in God's eternal kingdom.

The Glorious Mysteries invite believers to reflect on the triumph and glory that Jesus and Mary share. Through these meditations, one can contemplate the promise of eternal life, the outpouring of the Holy Spirit, the intercession of Mary, and the hope of heavenly glory. It is an opportunity to deepen faith, celebrate the triumph of Christ, and seek the intercession of Mary as Queen and Mother.

THE LUMINOUS MYSTERIES

The Luminous Mysteries, also known as the Mysteries of Light, are a set of meditations or events from the life of Jesus that were introduced by Pope John Paul II in 2002. These mysteries focus on key moments in Jesus' public ministry, highlighting His teachings and the manifestation of His divine nature. The Luminous Mysteries consist of the following five mysteries:

- The Baptism of Jesus in the Jordan: In this mystery, Jesus is baptized by John the Baptist in the River Jordan. As Jesus emerges from the water, the heavens open, and the Holy Spirit descends upon Him in the form of a dove. A voice from heaven proclaims, "This is my beloved Son, with whom I am well pleased" (Matthew 3:17).
- The Wedding at Cana: This mystery recounts the wedding feast at Cana, where Jesus performs His first public miracle. At Mary's request, Jesus transforms water into wine, revealing His divine power and affirming His role as the Son of God.
- The Proclamation of the Kingdom of God: In this mystery, Jesus preaches about the Kingdom of God and calls people to repentance and faith. He teaches through parables, heals the sick, and performs miracles, demonstrating the presence of God's reign among His people.
- The Transfiguration: This mystery portrays the Transfiguration of Jesus on Mount Tabor. Jesus, accompanied by Peter, James, and John, is transfigured before them, with His face shining like the sun and His garments becoming dazzling white. Moses and Elijah appear, representing the Law and the Prophets, and a voice from a cloud declares, "This is my beloved Son, with whom I am well pleased; listen to him" (Matthew 17:5).
- The Institution of the Eucharist: This mystery takes place during the Last Supper. Jesus institutes the Sacrament of the Eucharist, transforming bread and wine into His body and blood. He instructs His disciples to "do this in memory of me" (Luke 22:19), establishing the central act of worship in Christianity.

The Luminous Mysteries invite believers to reflect on the unique aspects of Jesus' public ministry and His divine nature. Through these meditations, one can contemplate His identity as the beloved Son of God, His power to perform miracles, His teachings about the Kingdom of God, His glorious transfiguration, and the gift of the Eucharist as a source of spiritual nourishment and unity with Him. It is an opportunity to deepen understanding of Jesus' mission and to seek guidance and inspiration in following His teachings.

ROSARY BEADS AND THEIR SIGNIFICANCE

Rosary beads are a tool used in prayer, particularly in the Catholic tradition, to aid in the recitation of prayers and the meditation on specific mysteries or events from the life of Jesus and Mary. They consist of a circular string or chain of beads with a crucifix or a medal attached at one end.

The beads on a rosary are organized into sets or decades, each containing ten small beads, usually separated by larger beads. These small beads are typically used to recite prayers such as the Hail Mary or the Our Father, while the larger beads are used for reciting the Glory Be or other prayers. The beads are meant to assist in keeping track of the prayers and provide a tactile and visual aid for focus and contemplation.

The significance of rosary beads lies in their practical and symbolic functions. Here are some key aspects of their significance:

Prayer Tool: Rosary beads serve as a practical tool for counting prayers. They help individuals maintain focus and rhythm during the recitation of repetitive prayers, such as the Hail Mary or the Our Father. The beads allow for a meditative and contemplative experience, providing a structured format for prayer.

Visual and Tactile Aid: The physical act of moving beads between one's fingers can help individuals enter into a prayerful state of mind. The touch and movement of the beads can serve as a reminder to stay present and focused on the prayer being recited. The visual presence of the beads also aids in maintaining concentration.

Devotional Symbolism: Rosary beads symbolize devotion and connection to God and the spiritual realm. They represent a visible and tangible reminder of one's commitment to prayer and faith. The crucifix or medal attached to the beads serves as a reminder of Jesus' sacrifice and the presence of Mary as an intercessor.

Mystical Tradition: The use of rosary beads has a rich history within the Catholic tradition. The practice of reciting prayers while counting beads can be traced back centuries. It is a part of a long-standing devotional practice that has been passed down through generations, connecting individuals to the wider community of believers.

Personal and Communal Prayer: The use of rosary beads facilitates both personal and communal prayer. Individuals can use them for private devotions and reflection, while groups can gather to pray the rosary together, fostering a sense of unity and shared spiritual experience.

Spiritual Discipline: The regular use of rosary beads can foster spiritual discipline and consistency in prayer. By incorporating the practice of praying the rosary into one's daily routine, individuals cultivate a habit of seeking moments of spiritual reflection and connection with God. The repetitive nature of the prayers allows for a deeper immersion in the mysteries and facilitates a contemplative state of mind.

Meditative Journey: The beads of the rosary can guide individuals through a meditative journey as they reflect on the different mysteries associated with each set of prayers. As one progresses through the decades, they can engage their imagination and immerse themselves in the events of Jesus' life or the virtues exemplified by Mary. This meditative journey helps individuals to deepen their understanding of the Gospel message and to apply its lessons to their own lives.

Source of Comfort and Solace: Rosary beads can provide comfort and solace during challenging times or moments of distress. Holding the beads and reciting the familiar prayers can bring a sense of peace and reassurance. It allows individuals to place their worries and burdens into the hands of God, seeking guidance, strength, and consolation.

Symbol of Faith and Tradition: Rosary beads carry deep symbolic and cultural significance within the Catholic faith. They represent a longstanding tradition of devotion and prayer, connecting individuals to the spiritual heritage of the Church. Through the use of rosary beads, believers feel a sense of continuity with generations of faithful who have found solace, inspiration, and spiritual growth through this practice.

Reminder of the Power of Prayer: Rosary beads serve as a tangible reminder of the power of prayer in the lives of believers. They symbolize the belief that through prayer, individuals can seek God's grace, find comfort, obtain forgiveness, and experience spiritual transformation. The beads remind individuals of the invitation to approach God in faith, trusting in His love and mercy.

In conclusion, rosary beads are more than a mere tool for counting prayers. They hold profound significance as a practical aid, a visual and tactile reminder, a symbol of devotion, a source of discipline and comfort, and a connection to the larger spiritual community. Through the use of rosary beads, believers are invited to deepen their prayer life, meditate on the mysteries of faith, and cultivate a closer relationship with God and Mary.

HOW TO PRAY THE ROSARY STEP BY STEP

Begin with the Sign of the Cross: Start by making the sign of the cross while saying, "In the name of the Father, and of the Son, and of the Holy Spirit. Amen." This gesture signifies our faith in the Holy Trinity.

Optional Opening Prayers: Some people choose to recite additional opening prayers such as the Apostles' Creed, the Our Father, and the Hail Mary. These prayers help to focus the mind and heart before proceeding to the main prayers of the Rosary.

Announce the First Mystery: Each set of mysteries (Joyful, Sorrowful, Glorious, and Luminous) is associated with specific days of the week. Announce the first mystery you will be meditating on. For example, "The First Joyful Mystery: The Annunciation."

Pray the Our Father: Begin each decade (set of ten prayers) with the Our Father. This prayer was taught by Jesus Himself and serves as a foundational prayer in the Rosary.

Pray the Hail Mary: Following the Our Father, recite ten Hail Mary prayers while meditating on the specific mystery announced. This prayer honors the Virgin Mary and seeks her intercession. After each Hail Mary, you may pause briefly to reflect on the mystery.

Pray the Glory Be: Conclude each decade by reciting the Glory Be, which gives praise and glory to the Holy Trinity. You can also add the Fatima Prayer, which was revealed during the Fatima apparitions: "O my Jesus, forgive us our sins, save us from the fires of hell, lead all souls to heaven, especially those in most need of Thy mercy. Amen."

Optional Reflection: Some people choose to reflect on a short Scripture passage related to the mystery being meditated upon. This reflection can help deepen your understanding and connection to the mystery.

Repeat Steps 4-7 for each decade: Repeat steps 4 to 7 for each of the remaining four decades, announcing the corresponding mystery before each set of prayers. You can use the same pattern of one Our Father, ten Hail Mary's, one Glory Be, and the optional Fatima Prayer for each decade.

Conclude with Prayers: After completing all five decades, conclude the Rosary with the Hail Holy Queen prayer and the Sign of the Cross. The Hail Holy Queen is a traditional Catholic prayer asking for Mary's intercession, and the Sign of the Cross reaffirms our faith in the Holy Trinity.

Optional Closing Prayers: You may choose to conclude with additional prayers, such as the Memorare or a personal prayer of gratitude and intentions.

Remember, the Rosary is a personal prayer, and you can adapt it to your preferences and needs. It is important to approach the Rosary with a spirit of reverence, focus, and reflection, allowing the prayers and mysteries to draw you closer to God and deepen your faith.

BENEFITS AND SPIRITUAL SIGNIFICANCE

Strengthening of faith and relationship with God is one of the primary benefits and spiritual significance of praying the Rosary. Here's a closer look at how the Rosary helps in this aspect:

❖ DEEPENING FAITH:

The Rosary allows individuals to engage in prayerful reflection on the life and teachings of Jesus and the mysteries of the faith. Through the repetition of prayers and meditation on the mysteries, faith is nurtured and deepened. The contemplation of Jesus' life and the truths of the Gospel help individuals grow in their understanding and belief in God's love, mercy, and plan for salvation.

❖ PERSONAL ENCOUNTER WITH GOD:

Praying the Rosary is an opportunity for a personal encounter with God. As one reflects on the mysteries and engages in the prayers, they create a sacred space to connect with the divine presence. It is a time to express love, gratitude, and surrender to God, fostering a deeper relationship with Him. Through the Rosary, believers experience God's grace and guidance in their lives.

❖ INCREASED TRUST AND SURRENDER:

The Rosary invites individuals to trust in God's providence and surrender to His will. In meditating on the mysteries, particularly those involving Mary's submission to God's plan, individuals are inspired to imitate her trust and openness. This leads to a strengthened reliance on God's wisdom and a willingness to surrender one's own desires and plans to His divine purposes.

❖ SPIRITUAL CONSOLATION:

Praying the Rosary can bring spiritual consolation and reassurance during times of difficulty, doubt, or spiritual dryness. Through the repetition of familiar prayers and the meditative focus, individuals find solace and peace in God's presence. The Rosary provides comfort, reminding believers that they are not alone in their journey but are supported by the love and care of God.

❖ INCREASED AWARENESS OF GOD'S PRESENCE:

The regular practice of the Rosary cultivates an awareness of God's presence in daily life. By setting aside dedicated time for prayer, individuals become more attuned to God's voice and leading throughout the day. This awareness leads to a heightened sensitivity to God's presence in both joyful and challenging moments, fostering a deeper relationship with Him.

- ❖ **STRENGTHENED VIRTUES:**

The Rosary is a means to grow in virtue and live a more Christ-like life. Through the contemplation of the mysteries, individuals are inspired to cultivate virtues such as faith, hope, love, humility, obedience, and perseverance. The repetition of prayers and reflection on the virtues exemplified by Jesus and Mary provides guidance and encouragement in the pursuit of holiness.

- ❖ **NOURISHMENT FOR THE SOUL:**

The Rosary offers spiritual nourishment, feeding the soul with God's word, the mysteries of faith, and the virtues displayed by Jesus and Mary. It provides a source of inspiration, wisdom, and encouragement in one's spiritual journey. Praying the Rosary regularly helps individuals stay connected to their faith, remaining rooted in the truth and grace of God.

- ❖ **RENEWED DEVOTION TO MARY:**

The Rosary is deeply intertwined with devotion to the Blessed Virgin Mary. By meditating on the mysteries alongside Mary, believers grow in their love and devotion to her as their spiritual mother. Mary's intercession and maternal care strengthen their faith and relationship with God, as she leads them closer to her Son, Jesus.

In summary, praying the Rosary contributes to the strengthening of faith and deepening of one's relationship with God. It nurtures trust, surrender, and awareness of God's presence. It brings spiritual consolation and feeds the soul with God's wisdom and virtues. Through the Rosary, believers experience an increased closeness to God and a profound encounter with His love and grace.

MEDITATIVE AND CONTEMPLATIVE ASPECTS OF THE ROSARY

The Rosary encompasses meditative and contemplative aspects that contribute to its spiritual richness. Here's a closer look at these dimensions:

❖ MEDITATIVE PRAYER:

The Rosary is a form of meditative prayer that engages the mind, heart, and imagination. As the prayers are recited, individuals enter into a state of quiet reflection and focus on the mysteries of the faith. The repetition of prayers, such as the Hail Mary and the Our Father, allows for a rhythmic and contemplative experience, creating a space for deeper connection with God.

❖ REFLECTING ON THE MYSTERIES:

The Rosary invites believers to reflect on specific events from the lives of Jesus and Mary, known as the mysteries. With each decade, individuals meditate on the significant moments of salvation history, including the Incarnation, the Crucifixion, the Resurrection, and more. This reflection provides an opportunity to internalize the lessons, teachings, and virtues exemplified in these events.

❖ ENGAGING THE IMAGINATION:

The Rosary encourages the use of the imagination to enter into the mysteries being contemplated. By picturing the scenes in one's mind, individuals can place themselves within the events, encountering Jesus and Mary in a vivid and personal way. This imaginative participation deepens the impact of the mysteries and helps individuals connect with the spiritual truths they convey.

❖ CONTEMPLATIVE SILENCE:

While the Rosary involves the recitation of prayers, moments of silence are also integrated into the practice. These pauses allow individuals to rest in stillness and open themselves to the promptings of the Holy Spirit. In this contemplative silence, they can listen attentively to God's voice, experience His presence, and receive insights or inspirations related to the mysteries being meditated upon.

- ❖ **A PATH TO INNER STILLNESS:**

The repetitive nature of the Rosary prayers, combined with the focused contemplation of the mysteries, creates an atmosphere conducive to finding inner stillness. As the mind becomes attuned to the rhythm of the prayers and the meaning of the mysteries, distractions diminish, and a sense of calmness is fostered. This inner stillness opens the door to deeper communion with God and facilitates spiritual growth.

- ❖ **ENCOUNTER WITH GOD'S WORD:**

The Rosary allows for an encounter with God's Word through the scriptural basis of its mysteries. By reflecting on the events from the life of Jesus and Mary, individuals immerse themselves in the truths of Scripture. This encounter helps them internalize the Word of God, deepen their understanding of the Gospel, and allow it to transform their lives.

- ❖ **CONTEMPLATING THE VIRTUES:**

The Rosary's meditative aspects provide an opportunity to contemplate the virtues exemplified in the mysteries. As individuals reflect on Jesus and Mary's actions, attitudes, and responses, they are inspired to cultivate these virtues in their own lives. This contemplation fosters personal growth in areas such as humility, obedience, compassion, forgiveness, and faith.

- ❖ **CULTIVATING PRESENCE AND AWARENESS:**

The meditative and contemplative nature of the Rosary nurtures the practice of being present in the moment and aware of God's presence. Through intentional focus on the prayers and mysteries, individuals develop a habit of attentiveness to the divine presence, both during the Rosary and in their daily lives. This cultivates a deeper sense of communion with God and a heightened awareness of His loving guidance.

In summary, the meditative and contemplative aspects of the Rosary invite believers to engage their minds, hearts, and imagination. Through reflection on the mysteries, imaginative participation, contemplative silence, encounters with God's Word, and contemplation of virtues, individuals experience a profound connection with God and a transformative journey of spiritual growth. The Rosary becomes a means to enter into deeper communion with God, seek His wisdom, and cultivate a contemplative stance in life.

PROMOTING INNER PEACE AND SERENITY

P raying the Rosary can be a powerful means to promote inner peace and serenity. Here's how it contributes to fostering a tranquil state of mind:

- ❖ **STILLNESS AND REPETITION:**

The Rosary's repetitive prayers and rhythm create an atmosphere of stillness and tranquility. As individuals recite the familiar prayers, such as the Hail Mary and the Our Father, the cadence of the words and the gentle repetition help to quiet the mind and bring a sense of calmness. This meditative aspect of the Rosary aids in clearing mental clutter and inviting a peaceful state of being.

- ❖ **FOCUSED PRAYER AND CENTERING:**

The Rosary provides a focused prayer practice that helps individuals center their thoughts and intentions on God. By engaging in the prayers and reflecting on the mysteries, attention is directed towards the divine presence. This intentional focus allows for a temporary release from external worries and distractions, fostering a sense of peace and serenity.

- ❖ **CONNECTION WITH GOD'S LOVE AND PRESENCE:**

Praying the Rosary deepens one's connection with God's love and presence. As individuals meditate on the mysteries, they encounter the profound truths of God's mercy, compassion, and saving grace. This awareness of God's loving presence brings comfort, assurance, and a sense of peace. The Rosary becomes a means to experience the inner peace that comes from knowing and being in communion with a loving and merciful God.

- ❖ **SURRENDER AND TRUST:**

The Rosary encourages individuals to surrender their concerns, fears, and anxieties to God. By contemplating the mysteries, especially those that highlight surrender and trust in God's plan, individuals are reminded of the importance of letting go and placing their trust in Divine

Providence. This surrender and trust alleviate the burdens of worry and promote a state of inner peace.

❖ REFLECTION ON VIRTUES:

The Rosary invites individuals to reflect on the virtues exemplified by Jesus and Mary in the mysteries. Contemplating these virtues, such as humility, obedience, forgiveness, and love, helps individuals align their lives with these ideals. Living in accordance with these virtues brings inner harmony and peace of mind.

❖ HEALING AND EMOTIONAL COMFORT:

Praying the Rosary can offer emotional comfort and serve as a source of healing. The Rosary provides a space for individuals to pour out their hearts, expressing their joys, sorrows, and concerns to God. This act of sharing with God fosters emotional release, comfort, and a sense of being understood and cared for. Through the Rosary, individuals find solace and experience the healing power of God's love.

❖ GRATITUDE AND CONTENTMENT:

The Rosary encourages the practice of gratitude and contentment. As individuals reflect on the mysteries, they are reminded of the many blessings received from God. This prompts a spirit of gratitude and contentment, focusing on what is present and acknowledging God's goodness. Cultivating an attitude of gratitude contributes to inner peace and a sense of fulfillment.

❖ CONNECTION TO THE COMMUNION OF SAINTS:

The Rosary connects believers to the Communion of Saints, the community of the faithful in heaven and on earth. By praying alongside Mary and the saints, individuals experience a sense of unity and support. This connection to the spiritual family provides comfort, encouragement, and an assurance that they are not alone in their journey, contributing to inner peace.

In summary, praying the Rosary promotes inner peace and serenity by providing a structured and meditative prayer practice. Through stillness, focused prayer, connection with God's love and presence, surrender, reflection on virtues, emotional comfort, gratitude, and connection to the Communion of Saints, individuals experience a deep sense of tranquility and harmony. The Rosary becomes a pathway to finding inner peace and a source of solace amidst life's challenges.

INTERCESSORY POWER AND THE ROLE OF MARY

The Rosary holds a profound belief in the intercessory power of Mary and acknowledges her significant role in the spiritual life of believers. Here's a closer look at the intercessory power of Mary and her role in the context of the Rosary:

- **INTERCESSORY POWER:**

The intercessory power of Mary refers to her ability to intercede with God on behalf of humanity. It is believed that Mary, as the Mother of Jesus and a faithful disciple, has a special closeness to God. She is seen as an advocate and helper who can bring the prayers and needs of believers before God, seeking His mercy, guidance, and blessings.

- **MODEL OF INTERCESSION:**

Mary's intercessory role is exemplified throughout the Bible, such as her intercession at the Wedding at Cana (John 2:1-11), where she presents the needs of the wedding party to Jesus. This act demonstrates her concern for others and her desire to assist in their needs. The Rosary acknowledges and draws upon this model of intercession, inviting believers to seek Mary's assistance in presenting their prayers and intentions to God.

- **THE HAIL MARY AND INTERCESSION:**

The prayer most commonly associated with Mary's intercession in the Rosary is the Hail Mary. By reciting the Hail Mary, believers ask for Mary's intercession, imploring her to pray for them and to bring their petitions before God. The Rosary recognizes Mary's special role as a powerful intercessor and highlights her willingness to help and intercede for all who turn to her in prayer.

- **TRUST IN MARY'S ADVOCACY:**

The Rosary fosters trust in Mary's advocacy by encouraging believers to turn to her with confidence. Mary is seen as a loving and compassionate mother who desires the spiritual well-being of her children. By seeking her intercession, believers place their trust in her ability to bring their prayers and needs to the attention of God, trusting in her maternal care and concern.

- **SPIRITUAL MOTHERHOOD:**

Mary is often referred to as the "Mother of the Church" and the "Mother of all believers." Through her spiritual motherhood, she extends her care and intercession to all who seek her help. The Rosary acknowledges Mary's role as a nurturing and guiding presence in the lives of believers, inviting them to turn to her as a source of comfort, guidance, and intercession.

- **UNITY WITH CHRIST:**

The Rosary recognizes that Mary's intercession is rooted in her close relationship with Jesus. As the Mother of Jesus, she has a unique connection to Him and His saving work. By seeking Mary's intercession, believers are drawn closer to Jesus and united with His divine grace. Mary's intercession is understood as a means to deepen the relationship with her Son and to align oneself with His will.

- **MEDIATION OF GRACE:**

The Rosary acknowledges Mary's role in the mediation of grace, through which she assists in the distribution of God's graces to believers. By seeking her intercession, individuals open themselves to the outpouring of God's blessings and the transformative work of the Holy Spirit. Mary's intercession is believed to bring about spiritual growth, healing, and the fulfillment of God's purposes in the lives of believers.

In summary, the Rosary recognizes and embraces the intercessory power of Mary. By seeking her assistance and intercession through prayers such as the Hail Mary, believers acknowledge Mary's role as an advocate and helper. They trust in her closeness to God, her maternal care, and her ability to bring their prayers and needs before Him. Through Mary's intercession, the Rosary fosters a deepened relationship with Jesus and a profound sense of connection to the spiritual family of believers.

VARIATIONS AND ADAPTATIONS OF THE ROSARY

CULTURAL AND REGIONAL DIFFERENCES

The Rosary has been embraced and adapted by different cultures and regions, leading to variations in its practice and expression. Here are some examples of how cultural and regional differences have influenced the way the Rosary is prayed:

- **LANGUAGE AND TRANSLATION:**

One of the primary ways the Rosary varies across cultures is through the use of different languages. Depending on the region, the prayers of the Rosary may be recited in the local language, allowing individuals to connect more deeply with the prayers and mysteries in their native tongue. Translations of the Rosary prayers have allowed for wider accessibility and participation in various cultural contexts.

- **INCORPORATION OF LOCAL CUSTOMS AND TRADITIONS:**

Cultural and regional differences have led to the incorporation of local customs and traditions into the Rosary practice. For instance, in some cultures, processions, hymns, or specific devotions to particular saints may accompany the praying of the Rosary. These additions reflect the unique spiritual expressions and traditions of the respective cultures.

- **MUSICAL ADAPTATIONS**:

Cultural variations have also influenced the melodies, chants, and musical accompaniment associated with the Rosary. Different cultures have developed their own musical traditions that harmonize with the rhythm and atmosphere of the Rosary. These musical adaptations add cultural richness and enhance the spiritual experience of praying the Rosary.

- **ARTISTIC DEPICTIONS AND ICONS:**

The Rosary is often accompanied by artistic depictions and icons of Jesus, Mary, and the mysteries. These representations vary across cultures and regions, reflecting distinct artistic styles, symbols, and devotional expressions. Icons and artwork associated with the Rosary often capture the cultural nuances and spiritual sensibilities of the respective communities.

- **REGIONAL MYSTERIES AND DEVOTIONS:**

Some cultures have incorporated regional mysteries or devotions into the Rosary practice. For instance, in Mexico, the Guadalupe Rosary highlights the apparitions of Our Lady of Guadalupe to St. Juan Diego. These regional variations honor specific cultural or religious events, providing a unique focus for meditation and intercession.

- **PRAYER CUSTOMS AND GESTURES:**

Cultural differences also manifest in the customs and gestures associated with the Rosary. For example, some cultures may have specific ways of holding the rosary beads or particular gestures performed during certain prayers. These customs and gestures reflect cultural traditions and contribute to a more personalized and meaningful prayer experience.

- **REGIONAL FEAST DAYS AND CELEBRATIONS:**

The Rosary is often associated with specific feast days and celebrations that vary across cultures and regions. These occasions may include processions, special liturgies, or communal prayer gatherings centered around the Rosary. These celebrations reflect the cultural and religious significance placed on the Rosary within particular communities.

- **REGIONAL DEVOTIONAL PRACTICES:**

Cultural and regional variations extend beyond the actual recitation of the Rosary. Certain regions may have unique devotional practices associated with the Rosary, such as novenas or specific spiritual exercises connected to the mysteries. These devotional practices may incorporate local customs, prayers, or devotions that reflect the spiritual heritage of the community.

In summary, cultural and regional differences have given rise to variations and adaptations of the Rosary. Through language, customs, music, art, and regional devotions, the Rosary takes on distinct expressions while maintaining its core essence. These variations highlight the richness and diversity of the global Catholic community, allowing individuals to connect with the Rosary in ways that resonate with their cultural backgrounds and spiritual traditions.

SPECIALIZED VERSIONS FOR SPECIFIC INTENTIONS OR OCCASIONS

The Rosary has been adapted and specialized for specific intentions or occasions, allowing individuals to focus their prayers on particular needs or circumstances. Here are some examples of specialized versions of the Rosary:

- **HEALING ROSARY:**

The Healing Rosary is a variation that emphasizes prayers for physical, emotional, and spiritual healing. It often incorporates specific prayers or intentions for those who are sick, suffering, or in need of restoration. The reflections and meditations within the Healing Rosary concentrate on seeking God's healing grace and intercession for individuals or communities facing various health challenges.

- **PRO-LIFE ROSARY:**

The Pro-Life Rosary centers around prayers for the protection of human life from conception to natural death. It includes specific intentions for the unborn, mothers, fathers, families, and those affected by the culture of death. The mysteries and meditations within the Pro-Life Rosary reflect on the dignity and sanctity of life and invoke God's mercy and protection for all vulnerable individuals.

- **ROSARY FOR PEACE:**

The Rosary for Peace focuses on prayers for peace in the world, peace in communities, and inner peace. It often includes intentions for conflict resolution, reconciliation, justice, and harmony among nations and individuals. The meditations and prayers of the Rosary for Peace invoke God's guidance, healing, and transformative power to bring about peace in various contexts.

- **ROSARY FOR VOCATIONS:**

The Rosary for Vocations is dedicated to praying for vocations to the priesthood, religious life, and the mission of the Church. It includes specific intentions for individuals discerning their calling and for the sanctification and perseverance of those already in vocations. The mysteries and prayers of the Rosary for Vocations seek God's guidance and blessing on those discerning and living out their vocational journeys.

- **WEDDING OR MARRIAGE ROSARY:**

The Wedding or Marriage Rosary is often used during wedding ceremonies or as a devotional tool for married couples. It focuses on prayers for the couple's unity, love, and strength in their marriage journey. The reflections and intentions within the Wedding or Marriage Rosary highlight the virtues of love, commitment, fidelity, and mutual support.

- **ROSARY FOR THE DECEASED:**

The Rosary for the Deceased is a specialized version that centers around prayers for the souls of the departed. It is often prayed during funeral services or as a memorial for loved ones who have passed away. The meditations and intentions within the Rosary for the Deceased seek God's mercy, forgiveness, and eternal rest for the souls of the faithful departed.

- **ROSARY FOR SPECIAL INTENTIONS:**

The Rosary can be adapted for specific personal intentions, such as prayers for a loved one's healing, guidance in decision-making or spiritual growth. In these cases, individuals may incorporate personalized prayers or intentions within the framework of the Rosary, using its structure and meditations to focus their petitions and seek God's grace in their particular circumstances.

These specialized versions of the Rosary provide a framework for individuals to direct their prayers towards specific intentions or occasions. They allow for a more targeted and focused prayer experience, enabling believers to lift up their needs, concerns, and desires in a particular area of their lives. Through these adaptations, the Rosary becomes a powerful tool for intercession, reflection, and spiritual growth in various contexts.

POPULAR VARIATIONS IN DIFFERENT CATHOLIC COMMUNITIES

Different Catholic communities have developed popular variations of the Rosary that reflect their cultural and devotional traditions. Here are some examples of these variations:

- **DOMINICAN ROSARY:**

The Dominican Order has a particular devotion to the Rosary, and their variation is known as the Dominican Rosary. It emphasizes the importance of meditating on the mysteries while reciting the prayers. The Dominican Rosary includes additional prayers and intentions specific to the order, such as the Salve Regina (Hail Holy Queen) and the Litany of Loreto.

- **FRANCISCAN CROWN:**

The Franciscan Crown, also known as the Seraphic Rosary, is a variation attributed to St. Francis of Assisi. It consists of seven decades in honor of the Seven Joys of the Virgin Mary. Instead of the traditional five decades, it focuses on the joyful moments in Mary's life, such as the Annunciation, Nativity, and Assumption. The Franciscan Crown is often associated with Franciscan spirituality and devotion.

- **CHAPLET OF DIVINE MERCY:**

The Chaplet of Divine Mercy is a variation of the Rosary that emerged from the revelations to St. Faustina Kowalska. It involves the use of Rosary beads but follows a different format. Instead of the traditional mysteries, the Chaplet focuses on the Divine Mercy message and includes specific prayers, including the Divine Mercy Prayer: "Eternal Father, I offer you the Body and Blood, Soul and Divinity of Your dearly beloved Son, Our Lord Jesus Christ."

- **SEVEN SORROWS ROSARY:**

The Seven Sorrows Rosary is a devotional practice that focuses on the sorrows and sufferings of Mary throughout her life. It includes prayers and meditations on seven sorrows, such as the prophecy of Simeon and the Crucifixion. This variation aims to deepen the devotion and empathy for Mary's sorrowful journey and to seek her intercession for strength and consolation in times of suffering.

- **BRIGITTINE ROSARY:**

The Brigittine Rosary is associated with the Order of the Most Holy Savior, also known as the Brigittines. It consists of six decades, with each decade dedicated to one of the wounds suffered by Jesus during the Crucifixion. The Brigittine Rosary includes specific prayers and meditations on the Passion of Christ, invoking His mercy and love.

- **SCRIPTURAL ROSARY:**

The Scriptural Rosary is a variation that incorporates short Scripture readings related to each mystery. After reciting the traditional prayers, individuals read a corresponding Bible passage that highlights the mystery being meditated upon. This variation helps individuals engage more deeply with the Word of God and its connection to the mysteries of the Rosary.

- **MISSIONARY ROSARY:**

The Missionary Rosary is a variation that assigns different colors to each decade, representing different regions of the world. The colors correspond to the continents, and prayers are offered for the specific needs and challenges faced by the people of each region. This variation encourages global solidarity, awareness of missionary work, and intercession for the evangelization and well-being of all nations.

These popular variations reflect the diverse spiritual traditions and devotional practices within the Catholic Church. Each variation brings a unique focus and emphasis to the Rosary, enriching the prayer experience and allowing different communities to connect with the mysteries of faith in ways that resonate with their particular spiritual heritage.

COMMON QUESTIONS AND MISCONCEPTIONS

COMMON QUESTIONS AND MISCONCEPTIONS ABOUT THE ROSARY:

- Is the Rosary a form of idolatry?

No, the Rosary is not a form of idolatry. It is a prayerful devotion that involves meditating on the life of Jesus and seeking the intercession of Mary. The Rosary does not worship Mary or any other created being, but rather honors her as the Mother of God and asks for her prayers.

- Do Catholics worship Mary when they pray the Rosary?

No, Catholics do not worship Mary when they pray the Rosary. The Rosary is a form of devotion that seeks Mary's intercession, asking for her prayers and guidance. Catholics believe that Mary holds a special place in salvation history and serves as a powerful advocate, but worship is reserved for God alone.

- Why do Catholics repeat prayers in the Rosary?

The repetition of prayers in the Rosary, such as the Hail Mary and the Our Father, serves as a way to enter into a meditative and contemplative state. The repeated prayers provide a rhythmic and focused environment for reflection on the mysteries of the faith and foster a deeper connection with God.

- Is the Rosary just a superstitious practice?

No, the Rosary is not a superstitious practice. It is a rich tradition of prayer and meditation rooted in the Catholic faith. Praying the Rosary involves faith, trust, and devotion to God, seeking His grace and guidance through the intercession of Mary. It is not based on superstition but on a genuine desire to grow closer to God.

- Can non-Catholics pray the Rosary?

Yes, non-Catholics are welcome to pray the Rosary if they feel drawn to this form of prayer. The Rosary is a devotion that can be embraced by individuals from various Christian denominations who wish to engage in meditative prayer and reflect on the life of Jesus. It is a personal choice and can be a meaningful spiritual practice for anyone who desires to grow in their relationship with God.

- Is the Rosary mentioned in the Bible?

While the specific practice of the Rosary as we know it today is not mentioned in the Bible, the individual prayers and mysteries that make up the Rosary have biblical foundations. The Our Father (also known as the Lord's Prayer) is directly from the teachings of Jesus, and the Hail Mary incorporates passages from the Gospel of Luke. The mysteries of the Rosary are events from the life of Jesus found in the New Testament.

- Do you have to pray the Rosary to be a good Catholic?

Praying the Rosary is not a requirement to be a good Catholic. It is a popular devotion and prayer practice within the Catholic Church, but it is not obligatory. Catholics are encouraged to cultivate a personal prayer life and engage in a variety of spiritual practices that help them grow in faith and deepen their relationship with God.

- Is the Rosary just for older people?

The Rosary is not limited to older people. It is a prayer practice that can be embraced by individuals of all ages. While it may be more commonly associated with older generations, the Rosary is also prayed by young people, families, and individuals seeking a deeper spiritual connection. Its timeless nature and ability to foster reflection and contemplation make it relevant and accessible to people of all ages.

It is important to address these common questions and misconceptions about the Rosary to foster understanding and promote dialogue among individuals from various backgrounds and beliefs. The Rosary holds deep spiritual significance for many Catholics and provides a pathway to prayerful reflection, intercession, and a deeper relationship with God.

ADDRESSING COMMON DOUBTS AND CONCERNS ABOUT THE ROSARY:

- Repetition of Prayers: Some individuals may question the repetition of prayers in the Rosary, wondering if it becomes monotonous or lacks sincerity. It's important to understand that the repetition serves as a means of creating a meditative rhythm and focus. Each prayer is an opportunity to enter into deeper reflection and connection with God. The repetition allows the mind to become still, the heart to engage, and the words to resonate more deeply.
- Distraction and Lack of Focus: Many people struggle with distractions or difficulty maintaining focus during the Rosary. It's important to remember that distractions are a common challenge in prayer, and it's okay to acknowledge them without discouragement. When distractions arise, gently bring the focus back to the mystery being contemplated or the words of the prayers. With practice, it becomes easier to cultivate a more focused and attentive prayer experience.
- Time Commitment: Some individuals may feel overwhelmed by the perceived time commitment required to pray the Rosary. It's important to remember that the Rosary can be adapted to fit personal schedules and preferences. One can choose to pray a single decade, a full five decades, or spread it out throughout the day. The key is to find a rhythm that works best for individual circumstances and to make the Rosary a regular part of one's prayer life.
- Understanding the Mysteries: The mysteries of the Rosary can sometimes be seen as challenging to understand or relate to. It's helpful to remember that the mysteries are invitations to contemplate and enter into the life of Jesus and Mary. Reflecting on the events of their lives, even if not fully comprehended, allows for a deeper connection with the central truths of the faith. Over time, deeper insights and understanding can emerge through continued prayer and reflection.
- Balancing Devotion to Mary and Worship of God: Concerns may arise regarding the balance between devotion to Mary and worship of God. It's important to clarify that the Rosary does not replace worship of God, but rather serves as a means to deepen one's relationship with God through the intercession and example of Mary. The Rosary is a form of prayer that directs attention to God's saving work and seeks His grace through the assistance of Mary.
- Personalization and Authenticity: Some individuals may worry that praying the Rosary feels impersonal or that they are simply reciting words without personal meaning. It's crucial to remember that personalization and authenticity can be cultivated through active engagement with the prayers and mysteries. By reflecting on the meaning behind the words, applying them to personal circumstances, and opening the heart to the guidance of

the Holy Spirit, the Rosary can become a deeply personal and transformative prayer experience.
- Cultural and Denominational Differences: Doubts or concerns may arise due to cultural or denominational differences surrounding the Rosary. It's important to acknowledge and respect these differences while also recognizing that the Rosary holds universal elements that can resonate with people of diverse backgrounds. Engaging in open and respectful dialogue can help bridge these gaps and foster understanding.
- Addressing these doubts and concerns requires patience, open-mindedness, and a willingness to explore the Rosary with an open heart. Through continued practice, personal reflection, and seeking guidance from trusted spiritual mentors, individuals can find deeper meaning, connection, and spiritual growth in their Rosary prayer.

CLARIFYING MISCONCEPTIONS ABOUT THE ROSARY

- MISCONCEPTION: THE ROSARY IS A FORM OF WORSHIPING MARY.

Clarification: The Rosary is a prayerful devotion that honors and seeks the intercession of Mary, but it is not an act of worship directed towards her. The Rosary directs our prayers to God, with Mary serving as a guide and intercessor. Mary is venerated and honored as the Mother of God and a model of faith, but worship is reserved for God alone.

- MISCONCEPTION: THE ROSARY IS A SUPERSTITIOUS PRACTICE.

Clarification: The Rosary is a deeply rooted prayer practice within the Catholic tradition and is not based on superstition. It is a way to engage in meditative prayer, reflect on the life of Jesus, and seek spiritual growth. The Rosary encourages a personal relationship with God and fosters devotion, trust, and intercession.

- MISCONCEPTION: THE ROSARY IS ONLY FOR OLDER PEOPLE.

Clarification: The Rosary is for people of all ages, not just older individuals. While it may have been traditionally associated with older generations, the Rosary can be embraced by anyone seeking a deeper connection with God and a meditative prayer experience. The Rosary can be adapted to different stages of life and is a meaningful spiritual practice for individuals of all ages.

- MISCONCEPTION: THE ROSARY IS MONOTONOUS AND LACKS MEANING.

Clarification: The repetition in the Rosary is not meant to be monotonous but rather serves as a pathway to contemplation and deeper reflection. Each prayer and mystery invites individuals to engage their minds and hearts, leading to a more meaningful and personal prayer experience. The Rosary can be enriched by actively meditating on the mysteries and finding personal connections to the teachings and events of Jesus' life.

- MISCONCEPTION: THE ROSARY IS NOT BIBLICAL.

Clarification: While the specific practice of the Rosary is not mentioned in the Bible, the prayers and mysteries that make up the Rosary have biblical foundations. The Our Father and the Hail Mary incorporate direct passages from the Gospels, and the mysteries reflect significant events from the life of Jesus. The Rosary invites believers to reflect on the life and teachings of Jesus, which are rooted in Scripture.

- MISCONCEPTION: PRAYING THE ROSARY IS MANDATORY FOR CATHOLICS.

Clarification: Praying the Rosary is not mandatory for Catholics. It is a highly encouraged and cherished devotion within the Catholic Church, but individuals have the freedom to engage in various forms of prayer and spirituality. The Rosary serves as a powerful tool for personal and communal prayer, but it is not a requirement for being a good Catholic.

- MISCONCEPTION: THE ROSARY IS A SOLITARY PRACTICE.

Clarification: While the Rosary can certainly be prayed individually, it is also a practice that can be shared in community. Praying the Rosary with family, friends, or as part of a larger group can enhance the communal experience and foster unity in prayer. The Rosary can be a source of support, inspiration, and spiritual connection when prayed together with others.

By clarifying these misconceptions, we can foster a better understanding and appreciation of the Rosary as a prayerful devotion that invites believers to deepen their relationship with God, meditate on the life of Jesus, and seek the intercession of Mary. The Rosary is a rich and flexible practice that can be adapted to individual preferences and spiritual needs.

TIPS FOR PRAYING THE ROSARY EFFECTIVELY

CREATING A CONDUCIVE ENVIRONMENT FOR PRAYER

- ✓ Find a Quiet Space: Choose a quiet space where you can be free from distractions. It could be a dedicated prayer room, a corner in your home, or any place where you can find solitude. Eliminate or minimize noise and disturbances to create an atmosphere of stillness and peace.
- ✓ Remove Clutter: Clear the space of physical clutter and unnecessary items. A clean and organized environment can help create a sense of calm and focus. Consider using symbols or images that inspire you in your prayer, such as religious icons or artwork that holds personal significance.
- ✓ Set the Lighting: Adjust the lighting in a way that promotes a sense of tranquility. Natural light or soft, warm artificial lighting can create a peaceful ambiance. You may also consider using candles, which symbolize the presence of God and can add a gentle and contemplative atmosphere to your prayer space.
- ✓ Engage the Senses: Incorporate sensory elements to engage your senses and foster a deeper connection with your prayer. Soft instrumental music, calming chants, or gentle nature sounds can help create a peaceful backdrop. Consider using incense or essential oils with soothing scents that can aid in relaxation and concentration.
- ✓ Create a Focal Point: Set up a focal point for your prayer space. It could be a crucifix, an image of Jesus or Mary, a prayer altar, or a sacred text. Having a focal point helps direct your attention and symbolizes the presence of God, acting as a visual reminder of your purpose in prayer.
- ✓ Comfortable Seating: Choose a comfortable chair or cushion to sit on during your prayer time. Being physically at ease allows you to relax and focus more easily on your prayer. You may also consider using a prayer shawl or a small blanket for added comfort and warmth.
- ✓ Disconnect from Technology: Turn off or silence electronic devices that may cause distractions or interrupt your prayer. Disconnecting from technology helps you create a sacred space free from the distractions of phone calls, messages, and notifications.
- ✓ Establish a Ritual: Create a ritual that signals the beginning of your prayer time. It could be lighting a candle, reciting a specific prayer or mantra, or taking a few moments of silence to center yourself. This ritual helps transition your mind and heart into a prayerful state.

- ✓ Practice Mindfulness: Before you start your prayer, take a few deep breaths and consciously let go of any worries, anxieties, or distractions. Be fully present in the moment, bringing your attention to the present experience of prayer. This practice of mindfulness helps cultivate a deeper awareness of God's presence.
- ✓ Personalize Your Space: Make your prayer environment reflective of your personal spirituality and relationship with God. Add elements that hold special meaning to you, such as meaningful quotes, photographs of loved ones, or objects that remind you of important spiritual experiences or mentors.

Remember, the goal is to create an environment that nurtures your connection with God and supports a focused and meaningful prayer experience. Customize your prayer space according to your preferences and spiritual needs, adapting it over time to ensure it remains a conducive environment for prayer.

DEVELOPING A PRAYER ROUTINE

- ✓ Set a Time: Choose a specific time in your day that works best for you to engage in prayer. It could be in the morning, during a lunch break, or in the evening. Consistency is key, so select a time that you can commit to on a regular basis.
- ✓ Start Small: Begin with a manageable prayer duration that suits your schedule and comfort level. It's better to start with a shorter period of focused prayer that you can maintain consistently rather than setting unrealistic expectations. As you develop the habit, you can gradually increase the duration.
- ✓ Choose a Format: Determine the format of your prayer routine. It could involve structured prayers, meditation, contemplative silence, journaling, or a combination of different approaches. Find a format that resonates with you and aligns with your spiritual goals and needs.
- ✓ Find a Sacred Space: Designate a dedicated space for prayer where you can retreat and find solitude. It could be a room, a corner in your home, or a specific outdoor spot. Make it inviting and free from distractions to create an atmosphere conducive to prayer.
- ✓ Set Goals and Intentions: Identify specific goals or intentions for your prayer routine. It could be cultivating gratitude, seeking guidance, deepening your relationship with God, or interceding for others. Setting intentions helps bring focus and purpose to your prayer time.

- ✓ Use Prayer Aids: Utilize prayer aids such as prayer books, devotionals, spiritual readings, or guided meditation apps to assist and inspire your prayer routine. These resources provide structure, guidance, and fresh insights to enhance your prayer experience.

- ✓ Engage Your Senses: Incorporate sensory elements into your prayer routine to engage your senses. Light a candle, burn incense, play soft instrumental music, or surround yourself with natural elements like plants or flowers. These sensory cues can help create a prayerful ambiance.
- ✓ Establish Rituals: Develop rituals that signal the beginning and end of your prayer routine. It could involve lighting a candle, reciting a specific prayer, taking a few deep breaths, or making the Sign of the Cross. Rituals help transition your mind and heart into a prayerful state.
- ✓ Reflect and Review: Take time to reflect on your prayer experience. Journaling or noting down insights, thoughts, or answered prayers can help you track your spiritual growth and maintain a sense of gratitude and awareness of God's presence in your life.
- ✓ Stay Flexible: While routine is important, be open to flexibility and adaptability. Life's demands may require adjustments to your prayer schedule or format. Be gentle with yourself and adapt your routine as needed while remaining committed to the essential practice of prayer.
- ✓ Seek Accountability and Support: Consider sharing your prayer routine with a trusted friend or spiritual mentor who can provide encouragement, guidance, and accountability. Sharing your journey with others fosters a sense of community and strengthens your commitment to your prayer routine.

Remember, developing a prayer routine is a personal journey that requires commitment, discipline, and a genuine desire to connect with God. As you establish a consistent prayer routine, you will experience spiritual growth, deepened intimacy with God, and a greater sense of peace and guidance in your life.

TECHNIQUES FOR MAINTAINING FOCUS AND CONCENTRATION

- ✓ Set Intentions: Begin your prayer time by setting clear intentions and reminding yourself of the purpose of your prayer. This helps align your mind and heart, bringing focus to your conversation with God.
- ✓ Create a Distraction-Free Environment: Find a quiet space where you can minimize external distractions. Silence your phone, turn off notifications, and remove any potential sources of interruption. A dedicated and peaceful environment supports concentration.
- ✓ Use Visual Aids: Incorporate visual aids that help direct your focus during prayer. This can include religious artwork, icons, or a focal point like a crucifix. The visual elements serve as reminders and focal points to help anchor your attention.
- ✓ Engage Your Body: Use physical gestures or postures to enhance your concentration. You can kneel, sit upright with good posture, or hold your hands in a prayerful position. Engaging your body in prayer can help center your mind and promote attentiveness.
- ✓ Practice Deep Breathing: Take a few moments to engage in deep breathing exercises before and during prayer. Deep breaths help relax the body and calm the mind, allowing for increased focus and concentration.
- ✓ Repeat a Mantra: Choose a word or phrase that has personal meaning to you, such as "Jesus," "Peace," or "God's love." Repeat this mantra silently or aloud as you pray. The repetition of a focused word or phrase can help anchor your attention and ward off distractions.
- ✓ Embrace Silence: Allow for moments of silence in your prayer. Silence creates space for listening and attentiveness to God's presence. Embrace the stillness and use it as an opportunity to center your thoughts and deepen your connection with God.
- ✓ Use Guided Prayers or Meditation: Utilize guided prayers or meditation resources to assist in maintaining focus. These resources provide prompts and gentle guidance, helping you stay attentive and engaged in your prayer.
- ✓ Journaling: Keep a prayer journal to jot down any distractions, thoughts, or inspirations that arise during prayer. This act of acknowledging and releasing distractions can help refocus your attention on the present moment and the conversation with God.
- ✓ Practice Regular Prayer: Consistency is key in maintaining focus and concentration. Regular prayer establishes a rhythm and familiarity that allows you to enter into a more focused state more easily over time.
- ✓ Seek Spiritual Direction: If you find it challenging to maintain focus in prayer, consider seeking guidance from a spiritual director or mentor. They can offer insights, techniques, and encouragement tailored to your specific needs, helping you deepen your prayer experience.

Remember, maintaining focus and concentration in prayer is a skill that develops over time. Be patient with yourself and embrace these techniques as aids to support your prayer journey. As you persevere and cultivate a habit of focused prayer, you will experience greater spiritual growth, intimacy with God, and a deepened sense of presence in your prayer life.

PRAYING THE ROSARY

THE SIGN OF THE CROSS:

The Sign of the Cross is a simple prayer that involves making the shape of the cross while reciting the words. It is a way to begin and end prayers, invoking the Holy Trinity.

TO PRAY THE SIGN OF THE CROSS:

- Touch your right hand to your forehead while saying, "In the name of the Father."
- Move your hand to your chest while saying, "And of the Son."
- Touch your left shoulder while saying, "And of the Holy Spirit."
- Finally, touch your right shoulder while saying, "Amen."

THE APOSTLES' CREED:

The Apostles' Creed is a statement of faith that summarizes the core beliefs of Christianity. It is named after the belief that it reflects the teachings of Jesus' apostles.

TO PRAY THE APOSTLES' CREED:

Begin by saying, "I believe in God, the Father Almighty, Creator of Heaven and Earth; and in Jesus Christ, His only Son, our Lord, who was conceived by the Holy Spirit, born of the Virgin Mary, suffered under Pontius Pilate, was crucified, died, and was buried. He descended into Hell; the third day, He rose again from the dead; He ascended into Heaven, sits at the right hand of God, the Father Almighty; from there, He shall come to judge the living and the dead. I believe in the Holy Spirit, the Holy Catholic Church, the communion of saints, the forgiveness of sins, the resurrection of the body, and life everlasting. Amen."

THE OUR FATHER (THE LORD'S PRAYER):

The Our Father is one of the most well-known and widely used prayers. It was taught by Jesus to his disciples when they asked him how to pray.

TO PRAY THE LORD'S PRAYER:

Begin by saying "Our Father, who art in Heaven, hallowed be thy name; thy kingdom come, thy will be done on earth as it is in Heaven. Give us this day our daily bread, and forgive us our trespasses, as we forgive those who trespass against us; and lead us not into temptation, but deliver us from evil. Amen."

The Our Father can be found in the Bible in two places: Matthew 6:9-13 and Luke 11:2-4.

THE HAILS MARY:

The Hail Mary is a prayer that involves asking for the intercession of the Virgin Mary, the mother of Jesus.

TO PRAY THE HAIL MARY:

Begin by saying "Hail Mary, full of grace, the Lord is with thee; blessed art thou among women, and blessed is the fruit of thy womb, Jesus. Holy Mary, Mother of God, pray for us sinners, now and at the hour of our death. Amen."

The Hail Mary is not explicitly found in the Bible, but its roots can be traced to the greetings given by the angel Gabriel and Elizabeth to Mary in Luke 1:28 and Luke 1:42, respectively.

THE GLORY BE (THE DOXOLOGY):
The Glory Be is a short prayer praising the Holy Trinity.

TO PRAY THE GLORY BE

Begin by saying "Glory be to the Father, and to the Son, and to the Holy Spirit. As it was in the beginning, is now, and ever shall be, world without end. Amen."

ROSARY MYSTERIES

The Rosary mysteries are grouped into four sets known as the Joyful Mysteries, the Sorrowful Mysteries, the Glorious Mysteries, and the Luminous Mysteries. Each set consists of five mysteries, and when praying the Rosary, one typically meditates on one set of mysteries at a time. Here's a brief explanation of each set of mysteries:

JOYFUL MYSTERIES:

- ❖ The Annunciation: The angel Gabriel announces to Mary that she will conceive the Son of God.
- ❖ The Visitation: Mary visits her cousin Elizabeth, who is pregnant with John the Baptist.
- ❖ The Nativity: Jesus is born in Bethlehem, and Mary lays Him in a manger.
- ❖ The Presentation: Mary and Joseph present the infant Jesus in the temple.
- ❖ The Finding of Jesus in the Temple: Jesus, at the age of twelve, is found in the temple discussing with the teachers.

SORROWFUL MYSTERIES:

- ❖ The Agony in the Garden: Jesus prays in the Garden of Gethsemane before His crucifixion.
- ❖ The Scourging at the Pillar: Jesus is cruelly scourged by the Roman soldiers.
- ❖ The Crowning with Thorns: Jesus is mocked and crowned with thorns by the soldiers.
- ❖ The Carrying of the Cross: Jesus carries His cross on the way to Calvary.
- ❖ The Crucifixion: Jesus is crucified and dies on the cross for the salvation of humanity.

GLORIOUS MYSTERIES:

- ❖ The Resurrection: Jesus rises from the dead on Easter Sunday.
- ❖ The Ascension: Jesus ascends into heaven forty days after His resurrection.
- ❖ The Descent of the Holy Spirit: The Holy Spirit descends upon the apostles on Pentecost.
- ❖ The Assumption: Mary is taken body and soul into heaven by God at the end of her earthly life.
- ❖ The Coronation: Mary is crowned as Queen of Heaven and Earth.

LUMINOUS MYSTERIES:

- ❖ The Baptism of Jesus in the Jordan: Jesus is baptized by John the Baptist.
- ❖ The Wedding at Cana: Jesus performs His first public miracle by turning water into wine at a wedding.
- ❖ The Proclamation of the Kingdom: Jesus announces the coming of the Kingdom of God and calls for repentance.
- ❖ The Transfiguration: Jesus is transfigured before Peter, James, and John on a mountain.
- ❖ The Institution of the Eucharist: Jesus institutes the Holy Eucharist at the Last Supper.

When praying the Rosary, one typically begins by reciting the Apostles' Creed, followed by the Our Father, three Hail Mary's, and a Glory Be. Then, for each mystery, one recites an Our Father, ten Hail Mary's while meditating on the mystery, and a Glory Be. After completing the five mysteries, the Hail Holy Queen is prayed. The Rosary can be a powerful form of prayer and meditation, allowing individuals to reflect on the life of Jesus and seek the intercession of Mary.

FATIMA PRAYER

The Fatima Prayer, also known as the Decade Prayer, is a prayer inspired by the 1917 apparitions of the Virgin Mary in Fatima, Portugal. It is frequently recited at the conclusion of each decade of the Rosary. The following is the prayer:

- Begin by making the Sign of the Cross, invoking the Holy Trinity: "In the name of the Father, and of the Son, and of the Holy Spirit. Amen."
- Take a moment to center yourself and prepare your heart and mind for prayer.
- Recite the Fatima Prayer with reverence and intention:

> "Oh my Jesus, forgive us our sins, save us from the fires of hell, lead all souls to Heaven, especially those in most need of Thy mercy. Amen."

After praying the Fatima Prayer, you can take a few moments to reflect on the words and the meaning behind them. Consider the significance of seeking forgiveness, salvation, and intercession for all souls, especially those in greatest need of God's mercy. Finish by making the Sign of the Cross again: "In the name of the Father, and of the Son, and of the Holy Spirit. Amen."

It's important to approach the Fatima Prayer with a sincere and humble heart, truly desiring forgiveness, salvation, and the well-being of all souls.

CONCLUSION

In conclusion, we have explored various aspects of the Rosary, its structure, components, and significance in the Catholic tradition. We clarified common questions and misconceptions surrounding the Rosary, addressing concerns related to its practice and purpose. We discussed the benefits and spiritual significance of praying the Rosary, including its role in strengthening faith, promoting inner peace, and fostering a deeper relationship with God.

We highlighted the meditative and contemplative aspects of the Rosary, emphasizing the importance of focusing on the mysteries and engaging the senses during prayer. We also touched upon the intercessory power of the Rosary and the role of Mary as a guide and advocate.

Additionally, we examined the variations and adaptations of the Rosary, acknowledging the cultural and regional differences as well as specialized versions for specific intentions or occasions. We also discussed popular variations within different Catholic communities, showcasing the diverse expressions of devotion and spirituality.

Furthermore, we provided guidance on how to pray the Rosary effectively, including tips for creating a conducive environment, developing a prayer routine, and maintaining focus and concentration during prayer.

Throughout our discussion, we highlighted the significance of the Rosary as a powerful prayer tool that can deepen one's spiritual journey, foster a sense of peace and serenity, and cultivate a personal relationship with God. By engaging in the Rosary with reverence, intentionality, and authenticity, individuals can experience the transformative power of this ancient prayer practice.

The Rosary serves as a means to connect with the mysteries of the faith, seek God's grace, and find solace in the intercession of Mary. It is a timeless prayer tradition that continues to inspire and guide believers in their quest for spiritual growth, inner peace, and a deeper union with God.

As we conclude our discussion on the Rosary, I want to encourage you to embrace this beautiful spiritual practice in your own life. The Rosary offers a unique opportunity to enter into a deep and transformative encounter with God, guided by the loving intercession of Mary. It is a prayer that has been cherished by countless believers throughout history and continues to be a source of solace, strength, and spiritual growth.

Embracing the Rosary as a spiritual practice allows you to embark on a journey of faith, deepening your relationship with God and drawing closer to the heart of Jesus. Through the repetition of prayers and the contemplation of the mysteries, you open yourself to a profound encounter with the divine presence. The Rosary provides a framework for both structured prayer and contemplative reflection, enabling you to enter into moments of quietude, peace, and communion with God.

While initially it may seem challenging or unfamiliar, I encourage you to approach the Rosary with an open mind and a willingness to explore its depths. Start with small steps, dedicating a few minutes each day to prayerfully recite the prayers and meditate on the mysteries. Allow the rhythm of the prayers to guide you into a deeper state of contemplation and surrender.

As you persevere in this practice, you will begin to experience the spiritual benefits that the Rosary offers. You may find that your faith is strengthened, your heart is filled with peace, and your connection with God becomes more intimate. The Rosary has the power to transform your prayer life, drawing you closer to God's love, grace, and mercy.

Remember that the Rosary is not meant to be a mere recitation of words, but an invitation to enter into the mysteries of salvation, to walk alongside Mary as she ponders the life of her Son, and to seek her intercession in our lives. Allow the Rosary to become a sacred space where you can pour out your joys, sorrows, hopes, and struggles before God, trusting in Mary's maternal care and intercession.

Lastly, I encourage you to seek support and guidance from your faith community, spiritual mentors, or prayer groups. Surrounding yourself with others who share a love for the Rosary can provide encouragement, accountability, and a sense of camaraderie on your journey.

May the Rosary become a treasured part of your spiritual life, a source of solace, inspiration, and connection with God. Embrace this timeless prayer practice with faith, perseverance, and an open heart, and allow it to lead you closer to the heart of God, guided by the loving presence of Mary.

PRAYING THE ROSARY

THE SIGN OF THE CROSS:

The Sign of the Cross is a simple prayer that involves making the shape of the cross while reciting the words. It is a way to begin and end prayers, invoking the Holy Trinity.

TO PRAY THE SIGN OF THE CROSS:

- Touch your right hand to your forehead while saying, "In the name of the Father."
- Move your hand to your chest while saying, "And of the Son."
- Touch your left shoulder while saying, "And of the Holy Spirit."
- Finally, touch your right shoulder while saying, "Amen."

THE APOSTLES' CREED:

The Apostles' Creed is a statement of faith that summarizes the core beliefs of Christianity. It is named after the belief that it reflects the teachings of Jesus' apostles.

TO PRAY THE APOSTLES' CREED:

Begin by saying, "I believe in God, the Father Almighty, Creator of Heaven and Earth; and in Jesus Christ, His only Son, our Lord, who was conceived by the Holy Spirit, born of the Virgin Mary, suffered under Pontius Pilate, was crucified, died, and was buried. He descended into Hell; the third day, He rose again from the dead; He ascended into Heaven, sits at the right hand of God, the Father Almighty; from there, He shall come to judge the living and the dead. I believe in the Holy Spirit, the Holy Catholic Church, the communion of saints, the forgiveness of sins, the resurrection of the body, and life everlasting. Amen."

THE OUR FATHER (THE LORD'S PRAYER):

The Our Father is one of the most well-known and widely used prayers. It was taught by Jesus to his disciples when they asked him how to pray.

TO PRAY THE LORD'S PRAYER:

Begin by saying "Our Father, who art in Heaven, hallowed be thy name; thy kingdom come, thy will be done on earth as it is in Heaven. Give us this day our daily bread, and forgive us our trespasses, as we forgive those who trespass against us; and lead us not into temptation, but deliver us from evil. Amen."

The Our Father can be found in the Bible in two places: Matthew 6:9-13 and Luke 11:2-4.

THE HAILS MARY:

The Hail Mary is a prayer that involves asking for the intercession of the Virgin Mary, the mother of Jesus.

TO PRAY THE HAIL MARY:

Begin by saying "Hail Mary, full of grace, the Lord is with thee; blessed art thou among women, and blessed is the fruit of thy womb, Jesus. Holy Mary, Mother of God, pray for us sinners, now and at the hour of our death. Amen."

The Hail Mary is not explicitly found in the Bible, but its roots can be traced to the greetings given by the angel Gabriel and Elizabeth to Mary in Luke 1:28 and Luke 1:42, respectively.

THE GLORY BE (THE DOXOLOGY):

The Glory Be is a short prayer praising the Holy Trinity.

TO PRAY THE GLORY BE

Begin by saying "Glory be to the Father, and to the Son, and to the Holy Spirit. As it was in the beginning, is now, and ever shall be, world without end. Amen."

ROSARY MYSTERIES

The Rosary mysteries are grouped into four sets known as the Joyful Mysteries, the Sorrowful Mysteries, the Glorious Mysteries, and the Luminous Mysteries. Each set consists of five mysteries, and when praying the Rosary, one typically meditates on one set of mysteries at a time. Here's a brief explanation of each set of mysteries:

JOYFUL MYSTERIES:

- ❖ The Annunciation: The angel Gabriel announces to Mary that she will conceive the Son of God.
- ❖ The Visitation: Mary visits her cousin Elizabeth, who is pregnant with John the Baptist.
- ❖ The Nativity: Jesus is born in Bethlehem, and Mary lays Him in a manger.
- ❖ The Presentation: Mary and Joseph present the infant Jesus in the temple.
- ❖ The Finding of Jesus in the Temple: Jesus, at the age of twelve, is found in the temple discussing with the teachers.

SORROWFUL MYSTERIES:

- ❖ The Agony in the Garden: Jesus prays in the Garden of Gethsemane before His crucifixion.
- ❖ The Scourging at the Pillar: Jesus is cruelly scourged by the Roman soldiers.
- ❖ The Crowning with Thorns: Jesus is mocked and crowned with thorns by the soldiers.
- ❖ The Carrying of the Cross: Jesus carries His cross on the way to Calvary.
- ❖ The Crucifixion: Jesus is crucified and dies on the cross for the salvation of humanity.

GLORIOUS MYSTERIES:

- ❖ The Resurrection: Jesus rises from the dead on Easter Sunday.
- ❖ The Ascension: Jesus ascends into heaven forty days after His resurrection.
- ❖ The Descent of the Holy Spirit: The Holy Spirit descends upon the apostles on Pentecost.
- ❖ The Assumption: Mary is taken body and soul into heaven by God at the end of her earthly life.
- ❖ The Coronation: Mary is crowned as Queen of Heaven and Earth.

LUMINOUS MYSTERIES:

- ❖ The Baptism of Jesus in the Jordan: Jesus is baptized by John the Baptist.
- ❖ The Wedding at Cana: Jesus performs His first public miracle by turning water into wine at a wedding.
- ❖ The Proclamation of the Kingdom: Jesus announces the coming of the Kingdom of God and calls for repentance.
- ❖ The Transfiguration: Jesus is transfigured before Peter, James, and John on a mountain.
- ❖ The Institution of the Eucharist: Jesus institutes the Holy Eucharist at the Last Supper.

When praying the Rosary, one typically begins by reciting the Apostles' Creed, followed by the Our Father, three Hail Mary's, and a Glory Be. Then, for each mystery, one recites an Our Father, ten Hail Mary's while meditating on the mystery, and a Glory Be. After completing the five mysteries, the Hail Holy Queen is prayed. The Rosary can be a powerful form of prayer and meditation, allowing individuals to reflect on the life of Jesus and seek the intercession of Mary.

FATIMA PRAYER

The Fatima Prayer, also known as the Decade Prayer, is a prayer inspired by the 1917 apparitions of the Virgin Mary in Fatima, Portugal. It is frequently recited at the conclusion of each decade of the Rosary. The following is the prayer:

- Begin by making the Sign of the Cross, invoking the Holy Trinity: "In the name of the Father, and of the Son, and of the Holy Spirit. Amen."
- Take a moment to center yourself and prepare your heart and mind for prayer.
- Recite the Fatima Prayer with reverence and intention:

> "Oh my Jesus, forgive us our sins, save us from the fires of hell, lead all souls to Heaven, especially those in most need of Thy mercy. Amen."

After praying the Fatima Prayer, you can take a few moments to reflect on the words and the meaning behind them. Consider the significance of seeking forgiveness, salvation, and intercession for all souls, especially those in greatest need of God's mercy. Finish by making the Sign of the Cross again: "In the name of the Father, and of the Son, and of the Holy Spirit. Amen."

It's important to approach the Fatima Prayer with a sincere and humble heart, truly desiring forgiveness, salvation, and the well-being of all souls.

www.ingramcontent.com/pod-product-compliance
Lightning Source LLC
Chambersburg PA
CBHW050237230526
45470CB00005B/1992